SAFE SCHOOLS: A HANDBOOK FOR VIOLENCE PREVENTION

Provided by

and a service of the Kentucky School Boards Association

RONALD D. STEPHENS

NATIONAL EDUCATIONAL SERVICE
BLOOMINGTON, INDIANA

Cover art by Bill Dillon

Printed in the United States of America

Printed on recycled paper

ISBN 1-879639-32-7

Table of Contents

About the Author 5

Foreword 7

Executive Summary 9

Objectives   **Safe Schools: A Handbook for Violence Prevention** 11

Chapter 1   **School Safety Overview** 13

Chapter 2   **Getting Started** 17

Chapter 3   **Conducting a School Safety Assessment** 21

Chapter 4   **Legal Considerations in Safe School Planning** 29

Chapter 5   **Safe School Strategies** 37

Chapter 6   **Implementing the Plan** 51

Chapter 7   **Evaluating the Results** 55

Chapter 8   **Guidelines for Policy Development** 57

Appendix I   **Model Assessment Questionnaires** 63

Appendix II   **Sample Plans, Policies, Procedures, and Codes** 133

About the Author

Dr. Ronald D. Stephens currently serves as Executive Director of the National School Safety Center. His past experience includes service as a teacher, assistant superintendent, school board member, chief school business officer, and Vice President of Pepperdine University. He received his doctorate from the University of Southern California, and holds the California teaching credential, administrative credential, and the Certificate in School Business Management.

Dr. Stephens is a consultant and frequent speaker for school districts, law enforcement agencies, and professional organizations worldwide. He has appeared on every major television network, and on such programs as "The Today Show," "Good Morning America," "Donahue," "Oprah," and CNN. Additionally, he serves as the Executive Editor of *School Safety,* America's leading school crime prevention newsjournal.

Foreword

In this era of rising concern about how to create safe learning environments in our schools, *Safe Schools: A Handbook for Violence Prevention* is a welcome addition to the materials available on this vital topic. School leaders can turn to this handbook with the confidence that its practical and user friendly strategies will help them ensure school safety in the future.

I have long admired and endorsed the work of the National School Safety Center and its executive director, Ronald Stephens. His thoroughness in covering this subject in a down-to-earth style has created an informative and accurate tool that can easily be adapted to the concerns and issues unique to each school situation.

Safe Schools: A Handbook for Violence Prevention takes the reader through the critical steps in creating a safe school, including how to conduct a school site assessment, address legal and legislative requirements, and customize safe school strategies to meet the needs of his or her school community.

We must remember, however, that the success of safe school strategies will depend on the commitment and cooperation of **all** members of the community. A safe school plan cannot be effectively implemented without extensive community involvement. Stephens also addresses this key issue and does not overlook any of the key players, including students, parents, law enforcement officials, business and political leaders, and youth advocacy organizations. This outstanding publication thoroughly covers all the issues in the complex and frustrating challenge of ensuring a safe school environment.

—Robert Mahaffey
Director, Publications
National Association of
Secondary School Principals

Executive Summary

There has never been a more formidable time to be a school administrator than in the 1990s. Crime and violence have invaded far too many of our nation's schools. Nearly three million thefts and violent crimes occur on or near school campuses every year, according to the National Crime Survey. That's almost 16,000 incidents per school day or one every six seconds. Many of the former fistfights have been replaced by gunfights. Former fire drills are being supplemented by crisis drills and, in some cases, bullet drills. School administrators must be prepared for more than the academic challenges of teaching reading, writing, and arithmetic. They must be prepared to create a learning environment that supports the educational process. More than ever, administrators need to establish safe schools which support the learning and success of all children and those professionals who serve them.

This resource guide is designed to help school administrators accomplish five major goals:

- To assess their school climate by identifying their top school safety issues.
- To determine their safe school goals.
- To develop a plan for reaching their safe school goals.
- To build a support network for policy development, plan implementation.
- To assist in continuing evaluation.

Most school administrators and teachers do not have the opportunity to select the students they will teach or to design the facilities in which they will serve. The school administrator inherits the clientele, the setting, and the community, which dramatically affects the quality of school life. These factors have a significant impact upon the success of the teaching and learning process and underscore the need for such a resource.

While most schools are safer than the communities they serve, any form of school crime, whether it be assault, fighting, harassment, or intimidation, should not be tolerated. Creating safe, welcoming, and drug- and violence-free schools is essential. To make this happen, school safety must first be placed on the educational agenda. Each school administrator must then conduct a school site assessment to determine the top issues and concerns within his or her school and then work with a broad-based safe school planning team to develop a plan to address them. Safe school planning is an ongoing, comprehensive, and systematic process that focuses on the "art of the possible." The goal is to create and maintain a positive and welcoming school climate — free of drugs, violence, intimidation, and fear — where teachers can teach and students can learn.

The best safe school plans integrally involve the entire community. This guide offers suggestions on how to involve students, parents, law enforcement officials, business and community leaders, and a wide array of youth-serving professionals. Safe school planning should be an inclusive and cooperative activity that involves school stakeholders in the development of a safe school mission statement. Collectively creating clear expectations for what the school can be will help develop a sense of ownership and commitment.

Restoring our schools to the tranquil and safe places of learning they can be requires competence, commitment, courage, and care. This planning guide provides an array of promising options which have been successfully used by school districts around the country. There is, however, no one way to make schools safe and drug-free. Each situation is unique and requires the involvement of the local community. This guide can be most effective, in fact, when its information is adapted rather than simply adopted. Safe school planning is a process which can bring unparalleled dividends to the administrators who effectively pursue a community commitment toward safe schools.

This guide provides a review of the factors that affect school safety and suggests how to get started by creating a planning team. A special segment addresses how to conduct a school site assessment, focusing on what to do before the assessment begins, how to gather pertinent data, how to track and monitor school crime, and how to make your campus safer through good environmental design and sensible management and maintenance.

The law is at the heart of safe school planning. It defines what must be done and establishes the parameters of what may be done. Now that school administrators are aware that knives and guns are in their schools, the courts are asking: "What are you doing differently this year that you were not doing before?" School administrators who can report that they have conducted a school safety site assessment of their top issues, collaboratively developed a comprehensive safe school plan, provided staff training, and produced a series of new policies and procedures which support the safety and well-being of students and staff will be in a much stronger position to insulate themselves and their school systems from potential liability. More importantly, though, they will have made their campuses safer for everyone.

The policy guide closes with segments on implementation, evaluation, and policy development. Creating a safe school is certainly a compelling idea, but if safe school strategies cannot be clearly communicated and implemented, they are of no value. This planning guide focuses on key ways to put school safety concepts to work for you. Several appendices complement the work.

A safe school will not happen by accident. It is contingent upon continuing efforts and support from students, parents, staff, law enforcement officials, the courts, and all youth-serving professionals. Making commitments to invest time with children both at home and at school are two of the most important strategies that can be implemented. Making schools safe is a function of community will. These changes can occur when educational, supervisory, and environmental design strategies are combined with a deep care and appreciation for children. The process begins by placing school safety on the educational agenda and is maintained by a continuing commitment to the safety and success of all children. The rewards of an effective safe school plan will benefit students, staff, and the community by enhancing the safety and success of all children. This planning guide will help you start the process and keep you on the right track.

Safe Schools: A Handbook for Violence Prevention

This resource guide is designed to give the school administrator:

- The skills and knowledge necessary to develop, implement, and evaluate a comprehensive and systematic safe school plan.

- An understanding of the key elements involved in the safe school planning process.

- A knowledge of the key players and policy shapers who should be involved in the planning process.

- An awareness of the specific steps and activities involved in developing a safe school plan.

- The background and skills needed to conduct a school site assessment.

- A clear awareness of the legal aspects of safe school planning.

- An understanding of the important aspects of creating a positive school or classroom environment that strives to build self-esteem and self-confidence in school children.

- A vivid awareness of various school safety implementation and evaluation techniques and processes.

- A working knowledge of promising school safety ideas and strategies.

- A framework for developing safe school policies.

Chapter 1

School Safety Overview

Nearly three million thefts and violent crimes occur on or near school campuses every year, according to the National Crime Survey. That's almost 16,000 incidents per school day or one every six seconds.

Even though the number of crimes on school campuses has remained about the same for the last few years, recent statistics indicate that crimes committed at school are more serious in nature, the age at which children are committing these crimes is becoming younger and younger, and the frequency of assaults is increasing. The level of school crime and violence reported in the annual National Crime Survey is comparable to the findings of the National Institute of Education's (NIE) *Violent Schools - Safe Schools* study conducted in 1978, the last in-depth national study on school crime.

According to the National Crime Survey's report on teenage victims, approximately 67 out of every 1,000 teenagers experience a violent crime each year, compared to 26 violent crimes for every 1,000 persons age 20 or over. Teens also experience twice as many thefts as adults. About 118 out of every 1,000 teens were the victim of a theft annually, while the rate for adults was 62 per 1,000.

Twelve percent of the violent crimes in school buildings involved an offender with a weapon. In comparison, three times as many violent street crimes — 37 percent — involved a weapon. However, the National Crime Survey found that in other respects, violent crimes committed on the street or at school were similar in severity.

Perhaps there is no greater challenge today than creating safe schools. Restoring our schools to being tranquil and safe places of learning requires a major strategic commitment. It involves placing school safety at the top of the educational agenda. Without safe schools, teachers cannot teach and students cannot learn. Developing and implementing a safe school plan is a critical and essential part of this process. The strategies and concepts included in this guide are intended to reduce the opportunities for crime and violence in schools by promoting a safe school climate.

What is a safe school?
A safe school is a place where students can learn and teachers can teach in a warm and welcoming environment free of intimidation and fear. It is a setting where the educational cli-

mate fosters a spirit of acceptance and care for every child—where behavior expectations are clearly communicated, consistently enforced, and fairly applied.

A safe school campus is orderly and well maintained. Teachers and staff who care about the success of every child are at the heart of a safe school. Staff members are carefully selected and appropriately placed. Adequate adult supervision and parent and student involvement are key components of the school management process. A safe school campus is designed in a way that promotes natural supervision. Vibrant extracurricular programs and community activities are part of the overall sense of community and purpose.

Safe schools model high moral standards, send positive messages to the students, and demonstrate that the school community expects the best effort and performance from everyone. Learning and productivity are valued, and success is expected of everyone. Clear, positive academic expectations decrease the anxiety caused by vague academic standards and allow students to focus on the task of learning.

Factors that affect school safety

Factors that affect school safety include the environment of the surrounding neighborhood, drug activity, community crime rates, the presence of gangs or nonstudents on or around the campus, and school curriculum. Parent and community involvement, or lack thereof, also has a direct bearing on the campus climate. Facilities and their design can have a major impact on school climate. Many campuses were designed years ago and are difficult to supervise.

The quality of site leadership, including the principal's attitude, affects the campus climate perhaps more directly than any other single factor. A positive school climate begins with a principal who cares about students, knows how to show that care to them, and in-

spires teachers to demonstrate that same concern for students. Students not only care how much a teacher knows, but they know how much a teacher cares. Fostering an appreciation for students is one of the more important tasks a principal can accomplish.

School administrators are required to enroll virtually any student who shows up on their doorsteps. Oftentimes, students who have been in trouble elsewhere are shipped to new schools as a condition of probation. This is frequently referred to as an "opportunity transfer." School administrators deserve to know about the special needs and circumstances that these students bring to school so that appropriate education and behavior programs can be developed.

Six broad factors contribute to school safety. They include the personal characteristics of each student and staff member, the physical environment of the school, the social environment on campus, the cultural characteristics of the staff and students, the local political atmosphere, and the economic conditions of the surrounding community. A seventh factor, "community will," may sometimes transcend the other factors. Community will may well be the single most important factor that drives the nature, the structure, and the effectiveness of the safe school plan.

The personal characteristics of students and staff, the school's physical environment and the community's economic conditions are the "givens" which influence the school community. In contrast, school social environment, school cultural characteristics, and political components are more "malleable," meaning that they can be changed and improved through planning and action.

All individuals bring to the school setting a multitude of prior emotional, familial, and learning experiences that can positively or negatively affect their participation in the school process. For example, students who have been the victims of severe physical abuse or who have been raised in poverty present a unique challenge. These students often are extremely insecure and distrustful of new situations, and they may bring a sense of hopelessness and helplessness to the school community, altering the perceived safety of the school environment.

The personal characteristics of students and staff are unique dimensions of a safe school environment. They reflect the social and economic conditions of the surrounding community. These characteristics cannot be modified as can the other school environment dimensions. A goal of safe school planning is to develop an insightful understanding of how personal characteristics have a positive or negative effect on the other dimensions.

School culture is the collection of assumptions, expectations, and knowledge that students, parents, and staff have about how a school should function and how individuals in the school should act. It is made up of the beliefs and values that govern the day-to-day behaviors of everyone involved with the school, and it defines what is acceptable behavior at school.

The perception of belonging and commitment to the school that is felt by students and staff is an essential factor for school safety. How are individuals in the school treated? Is each individual treated with respect and dignity, or do students and staff withdraw from involvement out of fear that they will be ridiculed? A truly safe school has a shared sense of involvement and identification.

Safe school planning defined

Safe school planning is all about the "art of the possible." It is not limited by special restraints or a set of guidelines. Each community has the opportunity to shape the type of school climate it wishes to create. A safe school plan, more than anything else, is a function of community will, priorities, and interest. The components are limited only by the imagination, creativity, energy, and commitment of the local community. The key questions to ask are: "What is it we want to accomplish?" and "How do we want to make it happen?"

The best safe school plans integrally involve the entire community. Students, parents, law enforcement, mental health, business and community leaders, and a wide array of youth-serving professionals should be involved in the process. Safe school planning is an inclusive and cooperative activity. All school stakeholders need to be involved in the development of a school mission statement. Collectively creating a living school mission statement, with clear expectations for what the school can be, helps develop a sense of ownership for all who walk through the door.

A safe school plan is an ongoing, broad-based, systematic, and comprehensive process. The goal is to create and maintain a positive and welcoming school climate that is free of drugs, violence, intimidation, and fear — a place where teachers can teach and students can learn in a climate which promotes the success and development of all students and those professionals who serve them.

Students enrolled in public schools have the right to attend campuses which are safe, secure, and drug-free. Several states are now beginning to recognize the need for safe schools by passing legislation which either mandates or recommends that every school develop a safe school plan. South Carolina was the first state in the nation to mandate safe school planning by adding Section 59-5-65 to the state's Schoolhouse Safety Alliance Act of 1994. The Act required the State Board of Education to develop a model safe schools checklist to be used by districts to assess their schools' safety strengths and weaknesses.

The California State Board of Education has endorsed the development of comprehensive plans for school safety, discipline, and attendance by every public school and district in the state. According to the board, the plan(s) should be developed as a part of ongoing district and school planning efforts and should be reviewed and updated on a regular basis. The plan should be developed cooperatively by parents, students, teachers, administrators, counselors, and community agencies and then be approved by the local school district governing board. School districts should establish working relationships with law enforcement agencies, service agencies, and parents that will provide safe and orderly schools, improve attendance, and expand services to students and parents.

Chapter 2

Getting Started

Establishing a safe school planning team

The first step in creating a safe school plan is to establish a "Safe Schools Team." This group should involve a wide variety of key individuals within the community who touch the lives of children. Examples of critical team players include the superintendent of schools, chief of police, presiding juvenile judge, chief probation officer, prosecutor, health and welfare providers, parents, business leaders, mayor, city manager, church and community leaders, neighborhood service organization leaders, and representatives from mental health, corrections, parks and recreation, and emergency response teams, among others. Individuals who you believe may block the implementation of such a plan without their involvement should be included. Students should be at the heart of the process since they will provide tremendous insight and direction. The example from Savannah/Chatham County Public Schools provided on page 18 offers a model of what might be developed.

Planning structure and process

The safe schools team may be led by anyone in the community. In some communities, the pre-siding juvenile judge may be the key leader. In other areas, it may be the chief of police. Most generally, it will be the superintendent of schools. The safe schools team provides an excellent opportunity for the chief school officer to take an active leadership role in the community. At the site level, the school principal should take this leading role.

For any plan to succeed, the safe schools team must draw upon the cultural diversity of the community it represents. When the opportunity for including diversity is overlooked, the opportunity for developing wide-ranging solutions can be severely limited. Safe school planning initiatives are best established by community coalitions of school, law enforcement, and community leaders.

The following preliminary steps can facilitate the establishment of a safe school planning task force.

- Identify key players in the community who are willing and committed to serving on the safe schools team.
- Hold a communitywide meeting on school safety. All interested parties, including students and parents, should be invited to attend.

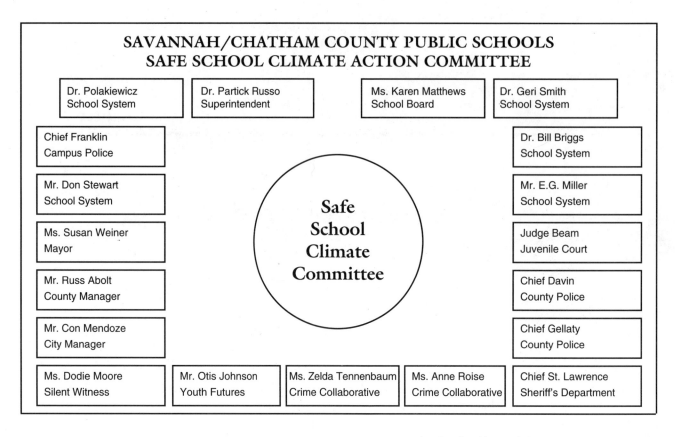

SAVANNAH/CHATHAM COUNTY PUBLIC SCHOOLS
SAFE SCHOOL CLIMATE ACTION COMMITTEE

Dr. Polakiewicz School System	Dr. Partick Russo Superintendent	Ms. Karen Matthews School Board	Dr. Geri Smith School System

Chief Franklin
Campus Police

Mr. Don Stewart
School System

Ms. Susan Weiner
Mayor

Mr. Russ Abolt
County Manager

Mr. Con Mendoze
City Manager

Safe School Climate Committee

Dr. Bill Briggs
School System

Mr. E.G. Miller
School System

Judge Beam
Juvenile Court

Chief Davin
County Police

Chief Gellaty
County Police

| Ms. Dodie Moore
Silent Witness | Mr. Otis Johnson
Youth Futures | Ms. Zelda Tennenbaum
Crime Collaborative | Ms. Anne Roise
Crime Collaborative | Chief St. Lawrence
Sheriff's Department |

Reprinted by permission
Savannah/Chatham County Public Schools
208 Bull Street
Savannah, GA 31401

In planning the community meeting, choose a date four weeks in advance. The letter of invitation to key persons within the community should state the purpose, date, time, and place of the meeting. The letter should offer a warm and personal invitation seeking their participation.

Before the meeting, do your homework by:

- Identifying the need for safe school planning.
- Approaching local law enforcement, juvenile justice and community leaders to solicit their support.
- Reviewing news clips, local crime reports and current literature in the area of school safety to gain a perspective on local community issues prior to the first meeting.
- Enlisting community support to create a climate for action.

Once the team is formed, members need to spend time educating themselves and the community about school crime and violence prevention. It is a good idea to choose two or three talented people from the team to undergo specialized training in violence prevention. They can then train other team members as well as members of the community.

Creating a timetable

Making the timetable and process work requires a specific agenda with bench marks and guidelines. Short of developing your own schedule, the following team agenda can help you get started.

Identifying program elements

When it comes to safe school planning, it is important to remember that it is an ongoing process. There is no specific formula that outlines everything that a safe school plan should entail. Rather, it is more appropriate to identify an array of potential areas that should be addressed. After the safe schools team is formed, members should begin to identify specific issues that they want to address in the safe school plan. These may include:
- Public awareness
- Curriculum focusing on pro-social skills and conflict resolution
- Behavior/conduct/discipline codes
- Campus supervision
- Crisis management and emergency evacuation
- Attendance
- Truancy prevention
- Drug prevention
- Interagency partnerships; youth-service networks
- Cultural and social awareness
- Student leadership
- Parent participation/involvement of senior citizens
- Special event management
- Crime prevention through environmental design
- Extracurricular activities and recreation
- School/law enforcement partnership
- Careful screening and selection of staff
- Violence prevention (pre-service and in-service training programs)
- School security
- Community service/outreach
- Corporate/business partnerships
- Media relations
- Health service
- Transportation
- Legislative outreach and contact
- Evaluation and monitoring
- A restitution plan

Political and practical considerations

The politics of school safety can be very delicate and yet turbulent. As a wide diversity of team members come together, each person and group they represent must be made to feel that they are equally important. The safe schools team will be no better than the example set by its chair. The following ideas can help the school administrator survive and even thrive on the process.

- Rise above the politics. Emphasize a safe and welcoming environment for all children. Focus on the positive. Set goals using positive terms. For example, rather than focusing on combatting violence, state the goal in terms of developing safe schools. The goals are nearly identical, but the semantics cast the goal into positive perspectives.

- Be aware of special interest groups. They need to be heard and fairly represented, yet their influence must be balanced within the larger group structure.

- Recognize that safe school planning is like a marriage — it requires a lot of cooperation.

- Do not underestimate the value or influence of any member of the school safety task force or safe schools team. Make a special effort to accept, appreciate, and work with each participant. (Be especially careful to avoid underestimating school board members.)

- Determine in advance the amount of decision-making authority to be held by the safe schools planning team. Do they have the authority to make recommendations or decisions? Communicate this to team members before they decide to serve.

- Do not attempt to force particular decisions upon the group. Do not have hidden agendas which require only the committee's rubber stamp of approval.

- Realize that most issues being considered do not require immediate decisions. Invest the proper amount of time and energy necessary to carefully consider and develop a positive decision.

Chapter 3

Conducting a School Safety Assessment

Before the assessment process

In preparation for the assessment process, several resources should be gathered for the assessment team to review:

- All security and safety-related policies of the district
- A floor plan of school buildings
- A site plan showing the campus boundaries and access points
- School crime reports for the previous year
- Known safety and security concerns of the staff and students
- The school's media file of previous news coverage
- Log of police "calls for service" generated from the school or dispatched to the school
- Student handbook
- Teacher handbook
- Union contracts
- Disciplinary files
- PTA newsletters that address safety and security

Collecting data

An initial component of the safe school planning process is to determine the condition of the school with regard to a variety of safety issues, including violence and intimidation, weapons in school, gangs, substance abuse, harassment, and such seemingly minor behaviors as bullying and name-calling. Your candid self-appraisal of your top concerns will drive the development of specific safe school planning components and strategies. Safe school planning involves asking, "What type of behavior and learning climate do we wish to create, and what type of behavior do we wish to avoid?"

There should be at least four components in the assessment process. First, every school should have a comprehensive and systematic school crime reporting process through which written records are maintained on school crime incidents. The report should provide for some means of crime analysis to determine the relation of incidents to other incidents and situations that may be occurring on the campus. Maintaining such records can serve as a valuable student management tool. It can assist the administrator in discipline record management, but more importantly, it can assist the administrator in developing appropriate behavioral and educational plans for students in need of special supervision and training.

These individual school crime reports should be folded into a broader system of statewide reporting. Florida has taken this kind of approach (see page 65). Florida's reports provide valuable insight as to what the top problems and issues are and enable administrators to develop appropriate strategies and tactics that respond to these issues.

At one middle school, administrators discovered that nearly every fight on campus involved a specific group of young ladies who were members of an alleged dance club. In reality, it was an emerging female gang. Requirements for membership included beating up a certain number of individuals, vandalizing teachers' cars, or having sex with a specific number of young men. By conducting an analysis of the reported crimes, school officials were able to see a pattern. After further investigation and with parental and community support, the administrators put a stop to the new gang and formed a legitimate dance club with a faculty sponsor.

A second component involves a site review. You may wish to ask some or all of the sample questions displayed in the box on the right. There are specific point values and school safety implications for each question. Once the values are calculated, they will provide an indication of safety-related issues at your school. In addition, astute school administrators should ask additional questions on critical issues that affect school climate.

Scoring and interpretation

Multiply each affirmative answer by 5 and add the total. A score of 0 to 20 indicate that there are no significant school safety problems at your school. If you have a score ranging from 25 to 45, you have an emerging school safety problem and should develop a safe school plan. A score of 50 to 70 indicates that there is a significant potential for school safety problems. A safe school plan should be a top priority. You are sitting on a ticking time bomb if your score is over 70. Begin working on your safe school plan immediately, and be sure to get some outside help.

School Crime Assessment Tool

1. Has your community crime rate increased over the past 12 months?
2. Are more than 15 percent of your work order repairs vandalism-related?
3. Do you have an open campus?
4. Has there been an emergence of an underground student newspaper?
5. Is your community transiency rate increasing?
6. Do you have an increasing presence of graffiti in your community?
7. Do you have an increased presence of gangs in your community?
8. Is your truancy rate increasing?
9. Are your suspension and expulsion rates increasing?
10. Have you had increased conflicts over dress styles, food services, and the types of music played at special events?
11. Do you have an increasing number of students on probation at your school?
12. Have you had isolated racial fights?
13. Have you reduced the number of extracurricular programs and sports at your school?
14. Has there been an increasing incidence of parents withdrawing students from your school because of fear?
15. Has your budget for professional development opportunities and in-service training for your staff been reduced or eliminated?
16. Are you discovering more weapons on your campus?
17. Do you lack written screening and selection guidelines for new teachers and other youth-serving professionals who work in your school?
18. Are drugs easily available in or around your school?
19. Are more than 40 percent of your students bused to school without the option of choice?
20. Have you had a student demonstration or other signs of unrest within the past 12 months?

If the school site assessment questionnaire you use is insufficient to identify school safety issues and generate some action, a Risk Management Checklist may provide further opportunities to highlight needs in the safe school planning process (see page 121).

Survey students, teachers, parents, and staff

A third component of the assessment should involve a survey of teachers, students, parents, and staff members regarding behavioral and safety issues. The survey document should not only ask specific questions but also provide for some open-ended input. There are several questionnaire models which may be used to get the input of teachers, students, parents, and staff. The examples in Appendix I will provide an idea of some of the types of questions which may be used.

The fourth and perhaps most important component is to talk with students, individually and in focus groups. Typically students will not report their victimization to teachers, school administrators, law enforcement officials, or parents. If adults want to find out what is going on, they have to ask. The following questions are all excellent icebreakers: Are there areas of the campus you avoid? What type of initiation rites exist for new students? Are there ever any fights on this campus? What are the fights usually about? Are drugs easily available on this campus? Have you ever seen a weapon at school? The important thing is to get the students talking and establish a dialogue of trust. Students will offer some incredible insights.

Young people can provide an excellent reality check of what is happening. They can also suggest some excellent strategies for addressing their top concerns. The importance of including students in the review process was underscored by a student who told a particular administrator: "It's been a long time since you've been a kid, hasn't it, Mr. Preston?"

Another South Florida administrator, who was exasperated with a particular group of miscreants, called together the 12 top troublemakers in the school. He called this group the "Council of 12." He said to them, "Look, there is one thing we both have in common, you want to get out of this school, and I sure as h--- want you out of here, too. But the law says you have to attend school. To make this work, I need your help to make this campus a place where we all want to be and a place where we can work together to give everyone a fair and equal opportunity for education. I want you to work with me in creating and maintaining appropriate standards of behavior for courtesy, appearance, and overall student behavior."

By year's end, the "Council of 12" had made the transition from causing the problems on campus to being partners in resolving campus behavior issues. We not only get what we expect and deserve from students, but sometimes we also get the level of support we ask for. Students are valuable partners.

School crime tracking and record keeping

Schools and school districts vary in their methods of collecting and recording school incident data. School crime reporting laws typically require the site administrator to report the type and frequency of the criminal incident; a description of the crime; the age and sex of the offender and whether or not the offender is a student; where the crime occurred; if the individual is under school suspension or expulsion at the time of the offense; the age and sex of the victim and whether or not the victim is a student or school employee; the cost of the crime to the school and the victim; and what action was taken, among a variety of other questions which may have importance and relevance to the local school.

Some districts have sophisticated reporting and data recording procedures, including computerized systems. An incident report, however, may be as simple as recording information on a 3-by-5 index card. The important issue is that the following questions be answered:

- What happened?
- When did it happen?
- Where did it happen?
- Who was involved?
- What action was taken?

If the incident report requires answers to these questions, then school administrators will have the information needed to make informed decisions. Schools and districts that lack an organized and consistently applied data collection scheme are more likely to miss incidents and thereby underestimate and fail to respond to school crime data.

A set of standardized reporting forms and procedures provides for more accurate data and helps schools analyze crime problems. School crime statistics must be accurate if they will be used to develop an understanding of the most pressing safety issues confronting a school or district.

Examining security practices
The systematic collection and analysis of school crime data can be a powerful management tool to help schools maximize available personnel and reduce the vulnerability to violent acts within a school. Armed with accurate security incident data, a school district is prepared to discuss how it should respond to real incidents or the potential threat of violence.

Underlying all successful school security/ school police programs is one common theme: the need for a defined security department within the organizational structure. School security increasingly is an area of professional specialization within education. It cannot be conducted on an ad hoc basis. According to school security practitioner Peter Blauvelt, five basic options are available to any school district selecting a security response:
1. Do nothing.
2. Employ local police.
3. Contract with a guard service.

4. Hire security professionals.
5. Combine options 2, 3, and 4.

Each option has advantages and disadvantages. However, within these options or their appropriate combination will be a program that meets the needs of any school system.

A number of school districts do not need a formally organized security program. If a school system experiences little daytime crime, has few burglaries or acts of vandalism, and the local law enforcement agency responds quickly and effectively handles the few incidents that do occur, then it may not need a specially organized security operation.

In a school system where the presence of police officers is required, however, officers are needed to patrol school grounds, parking lots, hallways, and bathrooms; check student identification; handle trespassers, class cutters, and truants; investigate criminal complaints; deal with disruptive students; prevent disturbances at after-school activities; and conduct crime prevention and school safety workshops. Additionally, they may be needed to counsel students and faculty members on security issues. There are many advantages to employing local police:
- Personnel are trained.
- The size of the force can be increased or decreased as needs dictate.
- Radio communication is established.
- A pre-employment background investigation has been done.
- Officers have high visibility; personnel are uniformed and armed.
- Police have a high amount of prestige.
- In most large police departments, support personnel are available.
- Police power is extended beyond school boundaries.
- Little ambiguity exists about authority.

There are disadvantages:
- Officers are responsible to an authority other than the board of education.
- Police lack flexibility in dealing with delinquent acts.
- Personnel are armed and generally in uniform.
- The school has little or no input in selection of assigned personnel.
- The potential for violation of students' rights and resulting libertarian controversies exist.
- This option can be costly if schools must pay for police services.
- Turnover of personnel on school assignment can be high.

It is strongly recommended that a formal agreement be prepared which clearly states the duties and responsibilities of the police department and the school system.

Contracting with a guard service is often the first response schools take when attempting to respond to the public's demand that something be done to stop school crime and violence. Guard companies have been relatively successful where their primary objective has been to act as a deterrent to crime. But schools present a different set of demands, and the effectiveness of contracted guard service is suspect in a school setting if they function as the primary security response. There are many advantages of contracting with a guard service:
- Cost is low.
- The size of the force can be increased or decreased as needs dictate.
- School assignments and deployment are at the discretion of school authorities.
- School authorities have the right to dismiss unsatisfactory guard personnel.
- The school can determine how guards are dressed and whether they carry weapons.

There are disadvantages:
- Personnel are likely to be poorly trained.
- No pre-employment background investigations are conducted.
- Turnover of personnel may be high.
- Guards may lack insight into student problems.
- The contractor may employ marginal personnel who might be unemployable elsewhere.
- The contractor may inadequately supervise personnel.
- School personnel may have difficulty supervising and controlling the guards.
- A general disrespect for "Rent-a-Cops" may exist among students and others.
- The degree of the school's liability for misconduct or errors by guards may be uncertain.

Another option is to hire security professionals. A good school security or school police program could be expensive depending on the size and scope of the security operation. If the program's primary focus will be to deal with daytime, in-school incidents, then costs will be considerably less than a program focused on both daytime and nighttime operations. There are many advantages of hiring security professionals:
- The school system selects personnel.
- The personnel are responsible to the school system.
- The school system defines the role of security personnel.
- Duty assignments can be flexible.
- The school system has central control over the entire security program.
- An in-house response unit is available to meet crisis requirements.

There are disadvantages:
- The program must be budgeted a year in advance.

- It is difficult to increase force size quickly.
- Dismissal of personnel must follow established procedures, i.e., "with just cause."
- The program can be costly.
- A training program must be implemented.
- Schools often become overly dependent on security personnel, tending to involve them in administrative issues as well as security issues.

Schools and school systems vary. No one approach is going to meet every school's needs all of the time. Flexibility is the key to effective security. At times, a school will need to call on local police for support. Evening activities, particularly those events that attract large numbers of people and require parking control, often can be effectively handled by a contract guard service. It is relatively inexpensive and releases school security personnel to be on duty inside the event. Regardless of which option is selected, every school system needs to establish an office of school security with a competent person as the director or chief.

Reviewing the site and physical structures

Bring together key members of your safe schools team and walk the campus. The discoveries you make can be eye-opening and even quite remarkable. The Assessment Survey: Security Checklist on page 79 provides some questions you should ask and things you should look for. You are basically asking the question, "What can be done to make the campus safer?"

Crime prevention through design

Crime prevention through environmental design, or CPTED, is based upon the concept that the proper design and effective use of the environment can reduce the incidence and fear of crime. The underlying objective is to help schools attain their primary goal of educating children in a positive environment free of violence and fear. Reduced crime and vandalism

translates to more resources for learning, not only in economic terms. A safe school campus creates a psychological advantage for learning and positive behavior.

Crime prevention through environmental design has seven key components: access control, natural surveillance, formal surveillance, territoriality, defensible space, target hardening, and program interaction. When these seven components interact, campus crime and violence can be significantly reduced.

Access control

A basic concept of creating a safe school climate centers around controlling campus access. This means that either natural or formal components of access control must be in place. Many school administrators feel they can adequately control the students who are enrolled in their school; however, the big problems arise when nonstudents come on to the campus.

Addressing the "nonstudent" issue has several implications. First, the campus perimeter needs to be controlled. Second, the number of entrances and exits should be minimized. Directional flow is another aspect of access control. The campus should be designed so that visitors and guests must pass through a particular point or entrance. In other words, if the campus has several parking areas, those areas should be carefully controlled with limited access capability. Visitor parking should be easily identified with proper signage and set up in a way that visitor traffic, both pedestrian and vehicular, can be easily and naturally supervised from the main office or by security personnel.

Uniform visitor screening procedures should be in place on each campus. All visitors should be referred to the front office where they can be screened to ensure that they have legitimate business. Visitors should be asked such questions as: Who are you here to see? Do you have an appointment? Are you the authorized custodial parent?

Natural surveillance

Another key CPTED strategy is to move gathering areas to locations with natural surveillance and access control or to locations away from the view of the would-be offender. By designing formal gathering areas, informal areas become off-limits. Anyone observed in spaces that are not designated as formal gathering areas automatically will be subject to scrutiny. Illegitimate users will feel at greater risk and will have few excuses for being in the wrong places. Teachers and administrators will assume greater challenging powers through clear spatial definition.

Formal surveillance

After everything has been done to enhance natural supervision by removing architectural barriers and by keeping sight lines open through proper landscape maintenance, building design, lighting, and access control, the next major environmental factor includes formal supervision. It is important to create a high-visibility profile of administrators, faculty, and staff. However, before school administrators make duty personnel assignments, respective union rules and contractual agreements should be reviewed.

Duty personnel should be assigned to supervise high-incident areas. This is where the school crime report is critical. The report will suggest areas that need special supervision. Those areas may include the main entrance or campus perimeter, particularly if you are having problems with intruders. Restrooms and specific corridors are often key trouble spots. Stairways, locker clusters, and courtyard or commons areas frequently have similar problems. Student parking areas or other remote locations may generate additional risks. The main point is to identify high-incident locations and provide appropriate supervision.

When staff members cannot be everywhere at once, the school site may need to look at other more formal surveillance options. When the Las Vegas Unified School District realized it needed enhanced student supervision in specific campus areas, administrators went to an unlikely and yet creative source for help. They consulted with the security specialists at the local casinos. Casino officials advised the school on security equipment specifications, location, placement, management and system operation. The Las Vegas Unified School District now has one of the most sophisticated and best-managed surveillance programs of any public school system in the United States.

Territoriality

A specific objective of CPTED is to personalize space assigned to each person in order to emphasize the perception of ownership. This principle translates to the identification of territories within the school campus. Hallways, classrooms, and foyers are assigned to the "proprietors" of internal spaces — classrooms and offices. Responsibility for the general supervision and care of these territories goes with the ownership of the internal space. There should be a clear delineation of space as one moves through various areas of the campus. For instance, it should be clear when one is moving from the science wing to the fine arts wing or to the mathematics department. When space is clearly differentiated, it tends to be clearly territorialized and better controlled.

Defensible space

Numerous opportunities are available for environmental concepts to contribute to the productive management of schools. For example, one way in which CPTED principles can be applied is to provide clearly marked transitional zones that indicate movement from public to semi-public to private space. Multiple access points increase the perception that the school parking area is public and provide many escape routes for potential offenders. The use of barricades to close off unnecessary entrances during low-use times controls access and reinforces the perception that the parking area is private. As privacy expectations are enhanced, the space is perceived as more defensible by the regular user and is perceived as increasingly risky by the potential intruder.

Target hardening

Target hardening helps prevent crime. Target hardening asks the question, "What can be done to reasonably minimize the potential for campus crime without making the school appear to be a prison or fortress?" Effective target hardening maintains a balance between the development and implementation of appropriate security measures without being too draconian.

Careful planning should be devoted to identifying unacceptable risks and determining what degree of risk is acceptable. The objectives of target hardening include preventing the crime by making the criminal's objective difficult to attain; controlling the crime by slowing the criminal's progress and thereby increasing the chances of apprehension; and finally, by precluding additional crimes against the district. Once the word gets out that criminals will be caught, apprehended, and aggressively prosecuted, they will tend to look elsewhere for entertainment and challenge.

Program interaction

Effective program interaction implies that the facilities will be properly designed to enhance natural supervision. Problem areas will be supported by formal supervision. A close partnership will be developed among law enforcement and emergency service personnel. The staff and students will work together in creating defensible space and territoriality. The school's administration will take adequate steps to harden the target by minimizing criminal opportunities.

Assigned spaces should be designated and used for the type of activities expected. Effective CPTED can be achieved by placing safe activities in unsafe locations or placing unsafe activities in safe locations. This will enhance the natural surveillance of these activities by increasing the perception of safety for legitimate users and risk for

potential offenders. For example, student parking is an unsafe activity that is often located on the periphery of the campus and obscured by landscaping that minimizes natural surveillance. Try locating student parking in an area that has a direct line of sight from office windows, or try removing the block walls, trees, or landscaping that obscure natural surveillance.

Improve scheduling of space to allow for the most effective use. For instance, at lunchtime, conflict often occurs as groups attempt to go to the cafeteria while others attempt to return to class. It takes longer to get groups through the lunch line because of this congestion. In many schools, classroom and locker thefts occur during this period. Separating the cafeteria entrance and exit by space can help to define movement in and out of the area. Each group will arrive faster and with fewer struggles. Illegitimate users also will feel at greater risk of detection.

A successful application of these seven CPTED principles supports the concept that the proper design and use of physical space affects human decisions and behavior, leading to improved productivity and profit, with the by-product of loss prevention in a welcoming education setting.

Other strategies include:
- Overcoming distance and isolation through more efficient communication and design.
- Re-designating the use of space to provide natural barriers for conflicting activities.
- Providing clear borders for controlled space.
- Redesigning or revamping space to increase the perception or reality of natural surveillance.

Observation has shown that the design and use of school facilities have a direct relationship to code of conduct violations and criminal behaviors. One of the first steps in the design or redesign of school layouts is to conduct a CPTED assessment (see page 87 for a sample survey tool).

Safe Schools: A Handbook for Violence Prevention

Chapter 4

Legal Considerations in Safe School Planning

Establishing the legal framework

The law is at the heart of every major school safety issue today. One of the first steps in developing a comprehensive and systematic safe school plan is to look at the laws that pertain to school disorder. Their presence or absence will establish the legal framework from which to begin. Laws establish the parameters for "what is required" and "what may be allowed" in developing your plan. The law strives to articulate the reasonable standards that define the delicate balance between student rights and student responsibilities. Laws proclaim what must be done, imply what should be done, and establish limits for what may be done. Laws confer a code of professional expectations for school administrators and youth-serving professionals. Federal and state laws, as well as county and city ordinances, should be reviewed.

There are only three categories of individuals we require to be somewhere against their will. The first is prisoners. They are protected against "cruel and unusual punishment." The second category is the mentally insane. They enjoy the same protection. The third category is school children. They are seldom afforded the same protection. We require them to attend school in an encapsulated environment,

despite the high levels of crime and violence they may be forced to endure. If we are going to require young people to attend school, then we must provide an environment that is safe, secure, and peaceful.

The federal government has traditionally been silent in the area of education. However, increased federal spending for education has brought new requirements and conditions to the table. Recent court decisions have also contributed to the process. Federal guidelines exist in the area of information sharing and record keeping, search and seizure, and third-party liability. Legislation currently before Congress would require expulsion from school for certain weapons violations among students. The following are a few examples of federal laws that apply:

- The Federal Gun-Free School Zone Act of 1994 requires school officials who wish to receive federal funds to expel for a minimum of one year any student who brings, possesses, or uses a firearm on a public school campus.
- The Drug-Free Schools and Communities Act of 1986 (as amended in 1989) requires schools to provide alcohol-, tobacco-, and

other drug-use prevention programs to all students in all grades.

- The Americans with Disabilities Act prohibits discrimination against persons with disabilities or those who are perceived to be disabled, including those with HIV infection or AIDS, in public accommodations, employment, transportation, state and local government services, and telecommunications. (Schools are included in the state and local government services category.)
- Title VI of the 1964 Civil Rights Act prohibits discrimination on the basis of race, color, or national origin. The act states that no person shall be excluded from participation in, be denied the benefits of, or be otherwise subjected to discrimination under any program or activity receiving federal assistance from the Department of Education.
- Title IX of the 1964 Civil Rights Act prohibits discrimination on the basis of sex in any educational program or activity receiving federal financial assistance.

State laws should be carefully reviewed to determine what is required by state mandates relative to student behavior and management. As a minimum, the following codes should be reviewed:

- State Constitution
- Education Code
- Health and Safety Code
- Penal Code
- Child Welfare and Institutions Code
- Administrative Code
- Municipal Code
- School District Code
- Recent court decisions

The following is a sampling of Pennsylvania laws pertaining to school disorder and/or safety. These laws are provided and summarized for illustration purposes only. If your school is in Pennsylvania, you should examine the full text of the laws for specific language and requirements.

- 18 Pa. C. S. @ 912 (1993) *Possession of weapon on school property* — A person commits a misdemeanor of the first degree if he or she possesses a weapon in the buildings of, on the grounds of, or in any conveyance providing transportation to or from any elementary or secondary public, private school, or parochial school.
- 18 Pa. C. S. @ 2702 (1993) *Aggravated assault* — A person is guilty of aggravated assault, a felony of the second degree, if he or she "attempts to cause or intentionally or knowingly causes bodily injury to a teaching staff member, school board member, other employee, or student" of any elementary or secondary public, private, or parochial school "while acting in the scope of his or her employment or because of his or her employment relationship to the school."
- 34 Pa. C. S. @ 2505 (1993) *Safety zones* — Generally, it is unlawful for a person to discharge, for any reason, any firearm, arrow, or other deadly weapon within or through a safety zone. (Some exceptions apply.) A safety zone includes the area within 150 yards around any building or attached or detached playground of any school, nursery school or day-care center.
- 18 Pa. C. S. @ 3307 (1993) *Institutional vandalism* — A person commits the offense of institutional vandalism if he or she knowingly desecrates, vandalizes, defaces, or otherwise damages any school, educational facility, community center, municipal building, courthouse facility, or juvenile detention center. An offense under this section is a felony of the third degree if the act is one of desecration as defined in Section 5509 or if the actor causes pecuniary loss in excess of $5,000. Pecuniary

loss includes the cost of repair or replacement of the property affected. Otherwise, institutional vandalism is a misdemeanor of the second degree.

- 18 Pa. C. S. @ 6314 (1993) *Sentencing and penalties for trafficking drugs to minors* — If a person over 18 years of age is convicted for trafficking drugs and the delivery or possession was with the intent to deliver the controlled substance to a minor, he or she will be sentenced to a minimum of at least one year total confinement. In addition to the mandatory minimum sentence, the person shall be sentenced to an additional minimum of at least two years total confinement, if the person "committed the offense within 1,000 feet of the real property on which is located a public, private, or parochial school or a college or university."

- 24 Pa. C. S. @ 1-111 (1993) *Background checks of prospective employees; conviction of employees of certain offenses* — This statute requires that prospective employees of public and private schools submit with their employment application, a report of criminal history record information from prescribed sources. It also stipulates that no person shall be employed in a public or private school where the report of criminal history record information indicates the applicant has been convicted within five years immediately preceding the date of the report of any of the offenses listed in the statute.

- 24 Pa. C. S. @ 15-1547 (1993) *Alcohol, chemical, and tobacco abuse program* — Beginning with the school year 1991-1992 and each year thereafter, each public school student shall receive mandatory instruction in alcohol, chemical, and tobacco prevention abuse in every year in every grade from kindergarten through grade twelve.

- 42 Pa. C. S. @ 8337 (1993) *Civil immunity of school officers or employees relating to drug*

or alcohol abuse — Any officer or employee of a school who, in the scope of official duty, reports drug or alcohol abuse involving a student to a specified list of individuals shall not be liable for civil damages as a result of any negligent statements, acts, or omissions undertaken in good faith for the purposes set forth in this section.

Several Texas codes relate to safe schools and safe school planning. Examples include:

- Texas Education Code §21.702, *Content of Approved Programs,* and Texas Administrative Code §133.21, *Discipline Management Programs.*

- Texas Education Code §21.303, *Reports to Local Law Enforcements: Liability,* and Texas Education Code §21.3031, *Destruction of Certain Records.*

- Texas Education Code §21.936, *Child Abuse Reporting and Programs,* and Texas Family Code §34.02, *Contents of Report: To Whom Made.*

- Department of Justice, 28 *Code of Federal Regulations* (CFR) Part 35, *Nondiscrimination on the Basis of Disability in State and Local Government Services.*

- Texas Administrative Code §61.101 – 61.104, *School Facilities Standards.*

- Texas Education Code §21.174, *Public School Transportation System,* and Texas Education Code §21.181, *Contract with Transportation Company or System;* Texas Administrative Code §68.11, *Provisions of Services: General,* and Texas Administrative Code §68.32, *Operation of School Buses.*

- Texas Civil Statutes Article 5182b §295.1 – 295.7.

- Texas Education Code §21.909, *Protective Eye Devices in Public Schools.*

- Texas Education Agency (1989). *Planning a Safe and Effective Science Learning Environment.* Publication Number GE9 370 12. Austin, TX: TEA.
- Texas Education Agency (1989). *Art Education: Planning for Teaching and Learning.* Publication Number GE9 370 05. Austin, TX: TEA.
- Texas Education Agency (1982). *Guidelines for Theater Safety.* Publication Number FE3 452 06. Austin, TX: TEA.
- Texas Administrative Code §75.213(i), *General Operational Provisions;* Texas Administrative Code §78.1(b)(2), *Vocational and Applied Technology Education;* and Texas Civil Statutes Article 5182b §295.1 – 295.7.

At the local level, you should also review county and city laws. At the district level, review the established policies of the school board. In Hawaii, the board has identified prohibited student conduct, classified the various types of offenses, and offered a range of disciplinary actions which may be imposed. For example, within their school system, the following offenses are unlawful and carry relevant disciplinary actions.

Class A offenses — unlawful conduct
Assault
Burglary
Extortion
Murder
Possession or use of dangerous weapons
Possession or use of firearms
Possession, use, or sale of illicit substances
Property damage
Robbery
Sexual offenses
Terroristic threatening

Class B offenses — unlawful conduct
Disorderly conduct
False alarm
Gambling
Harassment
Theft
Trespassing

Disciplinary action for Class A & B offenses
Crisis suspension
Detention
Disciplinary transfer
Dismissal
Suspension (up to 10 days)
Suspension (11 or more days)

Class C offenses — department-prohibited conduct
Class cutting
Insubordination
Leaving campus without consent
Smoking, use of tobacco substances
Truancy

Class D offenses — school-prohibited conduct
Conduct prohibited by school rules
Possession or use of contraband

Disciplinary action for Class C & D offenses
Crisis suspension
Detention
Disciplinary transfer
Dismissal
Parent conferences
Referral to an alternative education program
Reprimand and warning
Suspension (up to 10 days)
Suspension (11 or more days)

Balancing student rights and responsibilities

The Bill of Rights and other constitutional amendments provide instructive guidance relative to student rights, responsibilities, and behavior expectations, defining what students can say, wear (dress code), and do (behavior code). The Constitution and Bill of Rights create a context for the safe school plan. The student code of conduct is perhaps the most critical element of the safe school plan and sets the parameters of student behavior.

Every school policy should be, and most often is, guided by constitutional provisions. For example, the Fourth Amendment defines the limits of reasonable search and seizure. These guidelines have a significant influence upon the administrator's duty and responsibility to provide a safe and secure environment for all students, while protecting the individual rights of each student in confiscating contraband such as weapons, drugs, alcohol, or other items prohibited by law and school policy. The Fourteenth Amendment compels school administrators to equally and fairly apply school rules and to provide a fair hearing and equal due process in connection to a major student infraction or allegation.

School law provides the fundamental underpinnings for every action, procedure, and policy developed by a school system. It defines not only "what" we do, but "how" we do it. Law has also played a defining role in third-party liability and school litigation, as well as in crime abatement strategies. The law defines victims' rights and shapes restitution guidelines. The law also defines a school administrator's operational flexibility to safely and prudently manage a school campus. The importance of promptly correcting hazardous conditions on school campuses is underscored by the law as well. It is the educator's role to develop and recommend for adoption new laws that will ensure the safety and success of all children and those professionals who serve them.

Individual student rights are protected in varying degrees by state and federal constitutions, laws, and court decisions. Responsibilities are less clearly defined, but they are as essential to ordered liberty as are student rights. Acting responsibly requires thoughtfulness, care, respect, and appreciation for others.

The Council of Chief State School Officers issued a statement of 11 guarantees to students, including the right to attend schools that are safe and secure and that demonstrate sustained forward progress. With such rights come increased responsibility and accountability. Every safe school plan should acknowledge and take into account these basic concerns. Examples of this creative tension between rights and responsibilities include those listed in the box on page 34.

A school traditionally has been considered to act *in loco parentis* for its students; that is, the school acts *in the place of a parent or guardian* and with almost the same rights, duties, and responsibilities. Under this theory, school officials could act as if they were parents/guardians and do anything they deemed appropriate for the supervision or betterment of students. Whether actions thus taken were wise or the aims worthy was a matter left solely to the discretion of school officials. The courts were not expected to interfere in the exercise of that discretion.

Applying the *in loco parentis* doctrine, a school had no specific duty to assure safe schools, although it has been suggested a school was expected under the doctrine to protect students from harmful and dangerous influences. Indeed, in the few states where the doctrine is applied in school safety cases, willful and wanton misconduct on the part of school officials must be established in order to recover damages. This is a difficult burden of proof.

The rights of parents, guardians, and schools have nevertheless been subject to the overriding interest of the state. The state, as

Student Rights and Responsibilities

Right: Obtain an education at public expense and participate in the school program. (This right also extends to handicapped, married, or pregnant students.)
Responsibility: Attend all classes daily and be on time. Pursue and complete courses of study prescribed by state and local authorities and select electives based upon interest and need.

Right: Receive the benefits of education programs without restrictions based on race, color, or national origin.
Responsibility: Take discrimination grievances to appropriate school officials according to the school's procedures.

Right: Benefit from any educational program, without sex discrimination.
Responsibility: Take any discrimination grievance to appropriate person according to the school's procedures.

Right: Attend classes in which teachers are providing proper learning environments, materials, and instruction and in which grades are fairly assigned.
Responsibility: Attend school until graduation from high school or until the age established by state law.

Right: Use school equipment, books, and materials.
Responsibility: Take care of them and return them upon request.

Right: Express opinions orally or in writing.
Responsibility: Express opinions in a respectful manner. Expressed opinions will not be malicious or slanderous.

Right: Be free from unreasonable search or seizure on school grounds.
Responsibility: Behave appropriately and lawfully to ensure a proper learning environment.

Right: Receive fairness in disciplinary procedures.
Responsibility: Cooperate with school staff in disciplinary cases.

Right: Submit a grievance with the appropriate school officials when accused of misconduct.
Responsibility: File the grievance at the proper level. First seek a remedy at the school site. If it is necessary, take the problem to the district level. If there is still no resolution, court action may be required.

Right: Have individual school records, files, and data kept confidential except for legitimate use.
Responsibility: Provide the school with accurate data as requested and arrange for the transfer of records when changing schools.

Right: Have access to confidential school records, files, and data by an authorized adult.
Responsibility: Examine confidential school records and request correction of inaccurate information.

Right: Expect schools to be a safe place for all students.
Responsibility: Assist and cooperate with school faculty, staff, and administrators who are responsible for providing safe schools.

---

parens patriae, or *guardian of minors*, may restrict parental discretion and impose specific school obligations. This authority has been used to require attendance at school, mandate curriculum, and impose behavior expectations.

Student disciplinary rules must conform with constitutional requirements. Indeed, if a rule violates constitutional law, it is invalid, even if the rule is pursuant to a statute or specific grant of power. In the school setting, certain common and fundamental rights often are implicated. Simply stated, the problem is to reconcile the liberty of the individual student with public, school, or student welfare.

The first 10 amendments to the United States Constitution protect individual liberties against invasion by the federal government. The equal protection clause of the Fourteenth Amendment protects these liberties against state impairment, which includes the schools.

To a large extent, the constitutions of most states reflect federal law and protect individual liberties as a matter of state law. Thus, what is said about the federal constitution also typically applies to state constitutions. In some instances, however, a state constitution may afford additional protections. California's constitution, for example, guarantees students and staff the right to safe schools.

It is appropriate to review some of the specific constitutionally mandated rights relevant to school discipline regulations.

One of the fundamental constitutional rights assured by the Fifth and Fourteenth Amendments is that no rule can deprive a person of liberty or property without due process of law. The United States Supreme Court and other courts consistently have refrained from defining "due process" with precision. Rather, these courts have followed the policy of determining each case, as presented, upon its own merits.

Substantively, due process prohibits regulations from being unreasonable, arbitrary, or capricious. It also requires the use of means of enforcement that bear a real and substantial relationship to the object of a relevant rule.

Procedurally, due process requires notice and an opportunity to be heard prior to depriving a person of a liberty or property interest. Student disciplinary rules most often will raise questions of procedural rights. For example, in the landmark case of *Dixon v. Alabama State Board of Education*, the Fifth Circuit Court of Appeals held that students require notice and the opportunity for a hearing before they can be expelled for misconduct.

Similarly, in *Goss v. Lopez*, the United States Supreme Court extended minimal due process protection to all students being suspended from a public elementary or secondary school for as few as 10 days. This due process, however, can be informal and may not need to be in writing. As the seriousness of the misconduct and the potential institutional response increase, more procedural formality will be required.

Another common or fundamental right is equal protection of the law guaranteed by the Fourteenth Amendment. As with due process, each case is determined upon its own facts. The general rule is that equal protection of the law is denied when a rule is applied differently to different persons, without rational justification, under the same or similar circumstances. Constitutional equality requires impartiality between persons similarly situated. For example, schools may erringly violate equal protection by imposing more stringent disciplinary sanctions to one racial group than are applied to another.

A common and fundamental right raised by the First Amendment of the United States Constitution is freedom of religion. Under its umbrella, no rule may be adopted respecting the establishment of religion or prohibiting the free exercise thereof. The First Amendment also protects freedom of speech and of the press. In the significant case of *Tinker v. Des Moines Independent School District*, the United States Supreme Court found, under the First Amendment, that, except in the context of school-sponsored publications, activities, or curricular matters, restraints on student newspapers and publications generally are prohibited. Extracurricular freedom of speech and of the press may be restricted only when their exercise materially and substantially would disrupt the work and discipline of the school, or where the facts might reasonably lead school authorities to foresee such disruption.

The U.S. Supreme Court, in its January 1988 decision in *Hazelwood School District v. Kuhlmeier*, clearly established the right of schools to control the content of school-sponsored publications, dramatic productions, and other expressive student activities. The Court found that the First Amendment rights of students to freedom of speech and expression are not as broad as those of adults in some instances. Although students do not shed these rights at the schoolhouse gate, the court declared that a school need not tolerate student speech which is inconsistent with its educational mission.

Another First Amendment right permits individuals to freely associate in order to further their personal beliefs. While rules affecting this right must be reasonable, courts have been inclined to uphold such rules as forbidding membership by students in fraternities, sororities, and other secret societies. A school may even require a signed statement to this effect prior to allowing a student to participate in extracurricular activities. Rights of association must be subordinated to the orderly conduct of classes and other curricular affairs on campus.

The Fourth Amendment prohibits unreasonable searches and seizures. In *New Jersey v. T.L.O.*, the United States Supreme Court held that this protection applies to searches conducted by public school officials. However, while students have a legitimate expectation of privacy, a search will be considered valid even if probable cause does not exist, if there was a reasonable suspicion at its inception that the search will discover evidence of a violation of a school rule or the law and the search was conducted reasonably. After determining that the Fourth Amendment applied to students, the court deciding the T.L.O. case outlined the standard of reasonableness that governs schools searches.

As school administrators develop their policies on search and seizure, it is important to delineate clear behavior expectations and to give students appropriate notice that lockers are school property and that their use represents a privilege, not a right. Further due process notice should be given that lockers and their contents (for reasons of health and safety) may be searched at any time.

The Fifth Amendment grants the right against self-incrimination. It has generally, although not uniformly, been held that students may be required to testify in student disciplinary proceedings because this right applies only to criminal cases.

It is important to make continuing reviews of state laws and district policies to ensure that they do not violate federal guidelines. Student behavior expectations along with the fair and consistent administration of the code is essential in creating a positive school environment where students feel respected, honored, and welcomed.

Safe School Strategies

Although there is no guarantee that a school will ever be completely safe from crime, school safety should always be a top agenda item. The general preventive security measures outlined below can reduce the likelihood of campus violence:

- **Control campus access.** Access points to school grounds should be limited and monitored during the school day. A single visitor entrance should be supervised by appropriately trained personnel. Visitors must sign in at the reception area and wear an identification pass. Delivery entrances used by vendors also should be checked regularly.

- **Enhance interagency cooperation.** Safe schools actively cooperate with community agencies. Campus security operations should be coordinated with local law enforcement agencies. Do local fire departments and police participate in safety reviews of the campus, make presentations to students and staff, and assist in responding to school security and safety crises? In addition, do community support agencies such as county mental health, child protective services, and juvenile probation agen-

cies actively work together to identify students who are potentially dangerous or may engage in illegal activity? Collaborative steps should be taken to protect the rights of students and staff while rehabilitating juvenile offenders.

- **Mandate crime reporting and tracking.** Creating a safe school campus requires continuous tracking and monitoring of school crime problems. Analyzing the when, where, why, and who of school crime incidents will provide information about campus locations, individuals, and times that may require enhanced supervision.

- **Create a climate of ownership and school pride.** Every student and staff member should feel like a key part of the school community. This can be accomplished by involving every person in the safe school planning process, including students, parents, teachers, and community leaders. Establish home-room areas for faculty and students. Encourage school-sponsored groups and clubs to take ownership of specific hallways, display areas, or other locations.

- **Establish a parents center** on each campus that recruits, coordinates, and encourages parents to participate in the educational process. Possible activities include helping supervise hallways, playgrounds, restrooms, or other trouble spots. Classroom visitation and participation in special events is encouraged. A special training program that outlines expectations and responsibilities for parents in volunteer roles can be particularly helpful.

- **Target troublemakers.** A small percentage of young people create most of the school problems. There is a growing trend among schools and juvenile-serving professionals to begin sharing information about the serious misbehavior of juveniles. In Sylmar, California, a junior high student nearly stabbed his teacher to death. The student had a long history of misbehavior, but no one at the school knew it because the juvenile justice system typically treats each juvenile as a first-time offender every time an offense is committed. The California state legislature decided to change the way business is done. Consequently, it passed Senate Bill 142 mandating that the principal inform the teacher of every student who has had a background of criminal misbehavior. This action implies that the court will notify the principal whenever a juvenile is adjudicated.

    A similar information-sharing law has been passed in Virginia, and such revisions are being considered in several other states. Such information must be carefully managed and shared only with those individuals who have a legitimate "need to know," such as teachers, counselors, and relevant supervisory personnel. Otherwise the offender could become stereotyped and the staff prejudiced. Once troublemakers are targeted, special educational and supervision plans can be set in place. The purpose behind information sharing is to prevent the youngster from further victimizing himself and others.

- **Make the campus safe and welcoming,** beginning early in the morning. School safety leadership begins at the top. There is no question that the best principals spend the majority of their time outside their offices. Staying in tune and in touch cannot be accomplished in a cloistered office. Begin the day by greeting students at the front door when they first arrive. Be present in the hall during class changes. Visit classrooms and attend special events. The way we begin the day has a significant effect on how we will finish it.

- **Establish a vibrant system of extracurricular programs.** School children need positive things to do. Without interesting and challenging activities, students tend to fill the void with negative activities. A safe school provides students with several options.

- **Get parents on your side.** School administrators cannot create safe campuses alone. They need parent power. Work with parents to convince them of your interest in their child's success.

- **Create an active student component.** Students should be actively involved in their own safety and in safety planning, including learning conflict resolution techniques. Involve students in planning and managing student events and programs. Student participation promotes responsible student development and maturity, enabling students to be a part of the solution versus being a part of the problem.

- **Incorporate life skills curricula** that focus on good decision making, responsible citizenship, and conflict resolution. Young people need to learn how to deal with conflict. School violence is the tangible expression of unresolved conflict. If we can help children identify and implement constructive conflict resolution techniques, our campuses can be made much safer. A curriculum that emphasizes courtesy and thoughtfulness will go a long way toward creating a more positive and effective campus life.

- **Provide adequate adult supervision.** Children need continuous responsible supervision. This may include teachers, administrators, parents, campus supervisors, or law enforcement officers.

- **Establish an ongoing professional development and in-service training program** for campus supervisors. This would include training techniques in classroom management, breaking up a fight, and handling disruptive parents and campus intruders. School site administrators must acquire "crime-resistance savvy" and take greater responsibility in working with the school board and district to implement site security programs.

- **Clearly separate mixed vehicular functions.** For instance, bus loading and unloading should be separate from parent drop-off and pick-up points. Delivery entrances, loading docks, and vendor parking should be clearly delineated. Visitor, staff, and student parking should be visibly defined. It is important to ensure that none of these functions conflicts with one another.

- **Establish a visitor screening procedure.** A school administrator is responsible not only for keeping kids away from trouble, but also for keeping trouble away from kids. Having an effective visitor screening and intruder control process will accomplish that objective. A task of the safe schools team is to identify what safety measures should be implemented and how they might be accomplished.

- **Establish a close law enforcement partnership.** Include law enforcers in your curriculum, supervision, and crisis planning. Some of the most effective school peace officer programs bring the officer in contact with children in the early grades and allow the officer to follow the students through elementary, middle, and high school. School peace officers can do some of their best work once they know the children.

- **Establish a crisis response plan.** Through responsible planning, many potential problems can be avoided. However, there are times when a crisis is unavoidable. A good crisis plan focuses on crisis prevention, preparation, management, and resolution. It will also identify community resources and agencies that serve students.

- **Provide adequate support and protection for victims.** Once a crime has been committed, victims need special attention and support. This may mean more than a single counseling session. It may involve referral to a community service provider or ongoing support by the district. One meeting with a traumatized student or staff member does not mean the problem is solved. Continuing support may be necessary.

- **Develop a comprehensive crisis management plan** that includes step-by-step procedures for the following types of crisis situations:

Campus Unrest	Utility Failure
Assault & Battery	Chemical Spills
Weapons Possession	Suicide
Drive-by Shooting	Hostage/Terrorist
Illness/Injury	Rape
Kidnapping/Abduction	Bomb Threats
Natural Disasters:	Molestation
Earthquake	Child Abuse
Flood	Child Neglect
Tornado	Homicide
Hurricane	Unauthorized
Tsunami	Vendors
Intruders	Search & Seizure
Vandalism & Theft	Sit-Ins
Fire	Falling Aircraft
Extortion	Vehicle Accident

- **Establish clear behavior guidelines.** Make certain that behavior guidelines are clearly communicated, consistently enforced, and fairly applied toward all students. Posting the guidelines in prominent places and working with the supervising staff to consistently enforce them are essential.

- **Establish clear and reasonable dress codes.** We tend to act the way we dress. Gang attire, dress styles, or clothing with a disruptive message or disruptive appearance should not be tolerated.

- **Provide close supervision and remedial training for the serious habitual offender.** Where feasible, require restitution and community service from the juvenile offender. Create a special supervision program for the repeat offender. This includes in-school suspension or a series of alternative schools within the district.

- **Create a partnership of youth-service professionals** who can support and augment the schools' efforts to minimize school crime and campus disruption. The partnership should include schools, law enforcement, health and human services, courts, probation, the prosecutor, department of parks and recreation, parents, and business and community leaders, among others.

- **Nuisance abatement.** Work with local officials to develop ordinances and regulations that deal with graffiti abatement, drug and gang houses, trash, or other unsafe neighborhood conditions that affect the school.

- **Regularly update staff on school safety plans.** School staff should be informed and regularly updated on safety plans through in-service training. The training should include not only the certified staff, but also classified staff, including part-time employees and substitute teachers.

- **Carefully screen and select new employees.** One of the most important decisions that parents and communities make involves deciding who will teach, train, coach, counsel, and lead their children. Keeping child molesters and pedophiles out of classrooms, schools, and youth-serving organizations is a major task. Responsible parenting and thoughtful leadership on the part of schools and other youth-serving agencies should provide enough reason to establish appropriate safeguards for keeping child molesters away from our children.

Increasing litigation against school systems and child-care providers has created a financial reason to conduct appropriate background checks to protect the safety of children. Many school systems and youth-service organizations have already faced multimillion-dollar lawsuits for their failure to appropriately screen, properly supervise, and/or remove employees who may be a risk to children.

Every school system and youth-serving organization should have clear policy guidelines and procedures to weed out individuals with a criminal background of misbehavior involving children. Any record-screening program must consider the rights of privacy and due process as well as the right to a hearing when disqualification is involved. But the screening program must also balance these rights with the rights of the individuals who will be assisted by the youth-serving professional.

This process should begin at the hiring phase to identify potential problem applicants. In addition, procedures should be set in place to appropriately monitor and respond to other problems that may emerge. Sample procedures, policies, and forms that should be considered in any record screening program are provided on pages 43-50.

- **Promote crime prevention through target hardening and environmental design.** Provide maximum supervision in heavy traffic areas. Provide public telephones in strategic locations with dial-free connections to emergency services. Relocate safe activities near typical trouble spots. For instance, consider relocating a counselor's office next to a corridor or locker bay where problems have been occurring. Conduct ticket sales or concession activities in or near problem areas. Eliminate obstacles, such as trash cans and architectural barriers, that block or inhibit the traffic flow, supervision, and surveillance. Use parabolic/convex mirrors in stairwells and other locations that require improved supervision.

- **Establish a systemwide communications process.** A school communications network should be established that links classrooms and school-yard supervisors with the front office or security staff, as well as with local law enforcement and fire departments.

- **Identify specifically assigned roles and responsibilities.** Specific policies and procedures that detail staff members' responsibilities for security should be developed. These responsibilities may include monitoring hallways and restrooms, patrolling parking lots, and providing supervision at before-school and after-school activities.

- **Educate students, staff, and faculty** about reducing opportunities for personal victimization. Most of the time when students or staff are at their highest risk of being victimized, no law enforcement officer is available. Developing personal crime prevention savvy is essential.

- **Identify resources.** Schools should develop a comprehensive list of local, state and national resource services that can complement the school's safety efforts. Telephone and contact information should be regularly updated. Such resources could include the organizations listed in the box at right.

National Organizations and Hot Lines	
Alcohol Abuse Addiction Information & Treatment	1-800-274-2042
Alcohol Abuseline 24-hour crisis center	1-800-733-3232
Cocaine Abuse Addiction Information & Treatment	1-800-274-2042
Cocaine Abuseline 24-hour crisis center	1-800-755-5353
Cocaine Help Life	1-800-COCAINE
Crack Abuse Addiction Information & Treatment	1-800-274-2042
Drug Abuse Addiction Information & Treatment	1-800-274-2042
Drug Violation Hot Line	1-800-553-3673
Just Say No Foundation	1-800-258-2766
National AIDS Hot Line	1-800-342-AIDS
National Council on Alcoholism 24-hour Hot Line	1-800-622-2255
National Institution on Drug Abuse Information and Referral Line, Monday–Friday, 9:00 am–3:00 am EST	1-800-662-HELP
National Sexually Transmitted Disease Hot Line	1-800-227-8922
Teen Runaway HOT LINE	1-800-621-4000
Teen Suicide HOT LINE	1-800-522-TEEN

SAMPLE RECORD SCREENING POLICY

POLICY STATEMENT:
Children and youth have been the victims of physical, psychological, and/or sexual abuse by professionals or volunteers employed to assist, educate, serve, monitor, or care for them. Those who victimize children or youth frequently do so on repeated occasions and seek employment or volunteer for activities that will place them in contact with potential victims. As an agency serving children and youth, it is the policy of this agency to use reasonable efforts to screen employees and volunteers in order to avoid circumstances where children or youth would be endangered.

SCREENING GUIDELINES:
In General:
All prospective employees and volunteers who would have contact with children or youth will be screened to determine from reasonably available background information whether they pose a material risk of harm to such children or youth because of past conduct or other factors that indicate a potential for physical, psychological, and/or sexual abuse to children or youth. As a requirement for consideration, applicants must cooperate fully with an investigation and provide fingerprints, information, or consents as may be necessary to conduct the investigation.

Conduct of Background Search:
Background searches are to be undertaken by individuals designated by the agency's chief administrative officer. Based on preliminary results of the background investigation, persons/volunteers may be offered temporary/probationary status. Before a person is offered employment or allowed to volunteer, the findings from the background search will be reviewed. Fees associated with a background investigation will be paid according to established agency guidelines and procedures unless otherwise stipulated.

If information from a background search is obtained that reflects or may reflect on a person's fitness for service as an employee or volunteer and the person is otherwise qualified for such service, the prospective employee or volunteer will be advised of the information and provided an opportunity to review, obtain correction of, and respond to the information obtained. The source of information will not, however, be provided when information was given to the agency with the understanding that the source would be confidential.

Information obtained by the agency should not be further disclosed beyond the multi-agency team and is for purposes of the agency only. Such information may be disseminated to other authorized youth-serving agencies who are legally entitled to receive such information by the local jurisdiction unless restricted by law.

Minimum Screening Requirements:
Background checks of employees and volunteers shall be made as required by any applicable statute or regulation. These statutes and regulations include:
[Reference applicable statutes or regulations.]

Background Searches:
Background searches may include investigations that appear to be appropriate given the circumstances. Examples include:
- Applicant references
- Federal, state, or local law-enforcement officials
- State or local license or certificate registration agencies
- Motor vehicle or driver's license records
- Interviews or inquiries of former employers, colleagues, community members, or others having knowledge of applicant
- Health records
- Newspapers
- Criminal court records
- Civil court records

SELECTION GUIDELINES:

In General:

No background information obtained from employee and volunteer screening is an automatic bar to employment or volunteer work unless otherwise provided by statute or regulation. Instead, information obtained will be considered in view of all relevant circumstances and a determination will be made whether the employment of or volunteering by the person would be manifestly inconsistent with the safe and efficient operation of the agency recognizing the need to protect children and youth from physical, psychological, and/or sexual abuse.

Required Disqualification:

No employee or volunteer will be employed or utilized who is disqualified from so serving by any applicable statute or regulation. These statutes and regulations include:
[Reference applicable statutes or regulations.]

Additional Considerations:

Although not barred by applicable statute or regulation, a candidate may be disqualified from a position based on background information obtained from employee and volunteer screening. Other conduct, matters, or things may warrant disqualification in order to reasonably protect children and youth from physical, psychological, and/or sexual abuse. An applicant's failure to provide requested information will result in automatic disqualification of the applicant.

Where information is considered relevant to a position, the circumstances of the conduct, matter, or thing will be evaluated to determine fitness. The circumstances considered may include, but are not necessarily limited to:

- The time, nature, and number of matters disclosed
- The facts surrounding each such matter
- The relationship of the matter to the employment or service to be provided by the applicant
- The length of time between the matters disclosed and the application
- The applicant's employment or volunteer history before and after the matter
- The applicant's efforts and success at rehabilitation as well as the likelihood or unlikelihood that such matter may occur again
- The likelihood or unlikelihood that the matter would prevent the applicant from performing the position in an acceptable, appropriate manner consistent with the safety and welfare of children and youth served by the agency

No Entitlement:

The failure of a background investigation to disclose information justifying disqualification of an applicant does not entitle the applicant to employment. Positions are filled on the basis of all qualifications and relevant employment considerations.

SUBSEQUENT INFORMATION:

Should any information be obtained reflecting on the fitness of an employee or a volunteer to serve after selection or commencing service, such information will be considered by the agency. This information will be evaluated in a manner similar to its consideration in the selection process. Where appropriate, the services of the employee or volunteer may be suspended or terminated, or other appropriate action may be taken. Providing false, misleading, or incomplete information by an employee or a volunteer warrants termination.

EFFECT OF GUIDELINES:

The agency does not assume by these guidelines any obligation or duty to screen applicants or undertake background searches beyond that which would be required by law without these guidelines. No person shall rely on the use of background searches or any particular level of searches by virtue of these guidelines.

[Insert agency name/logo/address]

AUTHORIZATION
TO RELEASE INFORMATION

REGARDING:

Applicant's name: _____

Applicant's current address: _____

_____

Applicant's social security number: _____

Agency contact person: _____

Authorization expiration date: _____

I, the undersigned, authorize and consent to any person, firm, organization, or corporation provided a copy (including photocopy or facsimile copy) of this Authorization to Release Information by the above-stated agency to release and disclose to such agency any and all information or records requested regarding me, including, but not necessarily limited to, my employment records, volunteer experience, military records, criminal information records (if any), and background information. I have authorized this information to be released, either in writing or via telephone, in connection with my application for employment or volunteer service at the agency.

Any person, firm, organization, or corporation providing information or records in accordance with this Authorization is released from any and all claims or liability for compliance. Such information will be held in confidence in accordance with agency guidelines.

This authorization expires on the date stated above.

_____   _____
Signature of Prospective Employee or   Date
Volunteer

_____   _____
Witness to Signature   Date

[Insert agency name/logo/address]

REQUEST FOR INFORMATION

TO:

RE:

Applicant's Name _____ Social Security Number _____

Dates of Employment _____ Immediate Supervisor _____

Our agency, [*insert name*], is requesting information regarding the above-mentioned applicant who is seeking a position. This agency serves children and youth and, accordingly, undertakes background investigations to determine whether the individual poses a risk of harm to those who would be served.

We are interested in receiving any information or records that would reflect on the applicant's fitness to work with children and youth. Please complete the attached Employer Disclosure Affidavit and return it to our agency at your earliest convenience. Although any information you wish to provide is welcomed, we are especially interested in any conduct, matter, or things that involve established, or a reasonable basis for suspecting, physical, psychological, or sexual misconduct with respect to children or youth.

You may receive a separate written or telephone request from our agency for an employment reference regarding the applicant. Please respond to each request independently.

With this request is an authorization executed by the applicant. This releases you from any liability for your reply, either in writing or via telephone.

Thank you for your assistance.

Very truly yours,

_____

Failure by your agency or organization to provide information requested may result in automatic disqualification of the applicant.

APPLICANT DISCLOSURE AFFIDAVIT
(Please Read Carefully)

Our agency screens prospective employees and volunteers to evaluate whether an applicant poses a risk of harm to the children and youth it serves. Information obtained is not an automatic bar to employment or volunteer work, but is considered in view of all relevant circumstances. This disclosure is required to be completed by applicants for positions in order to be considered. Any falsification, misrepresentation, or incompleteness in this disclosure alone is grounds for disqualification or termination.

APPLICANT:_____
Please print complete name and social security number.

The undersigned applicant affirms that I HAVE NOT at ANY TIME (whether as an adult or juvenile):

Yes	No	*(Initial if answer is yes or no and provide brief explanation for a yes answer below.)*
____	____	Been convicted of;
____	____	Pleaded guilty to (whether or not resulting in a conviction);
____	____	Pleaded *nolo contendere* or no contest to;
____	____	Admitted;
____	____	Had any judgment or order rendered against me (whether by default or otherwise);
____	____	Entered into any settlement of an action or claim of;
____	____	Had any license, certificate, or employment suspended, revoked, terminated, or adversely affected because of;
____	____	Been diagnosed as having or been treated for any mental or emotional condition arising from; or
____	____	Resigned under threat of termination of employment or volunteer work for

Any allegation, any conduct, matter, or thing (irrespective of the formal name thereof) constituting or involving (whether under criminal or civil law of any jurisdiction):

Yes	No	*(Initial if answer is yes or no and provide brief explanation for a yes answer below.)*
____	____	Any felony;
____	____	Rape or other sexual assault;
____	____	Drug/alcohol-related offenses;

Yes	No	*(Initial if answer is yes or no and provide a brief explanation for a yes answer below.)*
____	____	Abuse of a minor or child, whether physical or sexual;
____	____	Incest;
____	____	Kidnapping, false imprisonment, or abduction;
____	____	Sexual harassment;
____	____	Sexual exploitation of a minor;
____	____	Sexual conduct with a minor;
____	____	Annoying/molesting a child;
____	____	Lewdness and/or indecent exposure;
____	____	Lewd and lascivious behavior;
____	____	Obscene literature;
____	____	Assault, battery, or other offense involving a minor;
____	____	Endangerment of a child;
____	____	Any misdemeanor or other offense classification involving a minor or to which a minor was a witness;
____	____	Unfitness as a parent or custodian;
____	____	Removing children from a state or concealing children in violation of a law or court order;
____	____	Restrictions or limitations on contact or visitation with children or minors;
____	____	Similar or related conduct, matters, or things; or
____	____	Been accused of any of the above.

EXCEPT THE FOLLOWING:

(If you answered yes to any of the above, please explain. If there were no yes answers, write "none".)

Description   Dates

_____
_____
_____
_____
_____
_____

The above statements are true and complete to the best of my knowledge.

Date_____   Signature of applicant _____

Date_____   Signature of witness_____

EMPLOYER DISCLOSURE AFFIDAVIT
(Please Read Carefully)

Our agency screens prospective employees and volunteers to evaluate whether an applicant poses a risk of harm to the children and youth it serves. Information obtained is not an automatic bar to employment or volunteer work, but is considered in view of all relevant circumstances. This disclosure is required to be completed by former employers in order for the applicant to be considered.

APPLICANT:_____
        Please print complete name and social security number.

As an agent of the former employer of the undersigned applicant, I affirm to the best of my knowledge that the undersigned applicant HAS NOT at ANY TIME:

Yes	No	*(Initial if answer is yes or no and provide brief explanation for a yes answer below.)*
____	____	Been convicted of;
____	____	Pleaded guilty to (whether or not resulting in a conviction);
____	____	Pleaded *nolo contendere* or no contest to;
____	____	Admitted;
____	____	Had any judgment or order rendered against me (whether by default or otherwise);
____	____	Entered into any settlement of an action or claim of;
____	____	Had any license, certificate, or employment suspended, revoked, terminated or adversely affected because of;
____	____	Been diagnosed as having or been treated for any mental or emotional condition arising from; or
____	____	Resigned under threat of termination of employment or volunteer work for

Any allegation, any conduct, matter, or thing (irrespective of the formal name thereof) constituting or involving (whether under criminal or civil law of any jurisdiction):

Yes	No	*(Initial if answer is yes or no and provide brief explanation for a yes answer below.)*
____	____	Any felony;
____	____	Rape or other sexual assault;
____	____	Drug/alcohol-related offenses;
____	____	Abuse of a minor or child, whether physical or sexual;

Yes **No**   *(Initial if answer is yes or no and provide a brief explanation for a yes answer below.)*

____	____	Incest;
____	____	Kidnapping, false imprisonment, or abduction;
____	____	Sexual harassment;
____	____	Sexual exploitation of a minor;
____	____	Sexual conduct with a minor;
____	____	Annoying/molesting a child;
____	____	Lewdness and/or indecent exposure;
____	____	Lewd and lascivious behavior;
____	____	Obscene literature;
____	____	Assault, battery, or other offense involving a minor;
____	____	Endangerment of a child;
____	____	Any misdemeanor or other offense classification involving a minor or to which a minor was a witness;
____	____	Unfitness as a parent or custodian;
____	____	Removing children from a state or concealing children in violation of a law or court order;
____	____	Restrictions or limitations on contact or visitation with children or minors;
____	____	Similar or related conduct, matters or things; or
____	____	Been accused of any of the above.

EXCEPT THE FOLLOWING:

(If you answered yes to any of the above, please explain. If there were no yes answers, write "none".)

Description   Dates

_____

_____

_____

_____

_____

_____

_____

The above statements are true and complete to the best of my knowledge.

Date_____   Signature of applicant _____

Name_____   Title_____

Company_____   Address:_____

City/State/Zip_____   Phone_____

Chapter 6

Implementing the Plan

Creating community support

A safe school plan is no better than the level of community support for it. Creating community support for safe schools is related to getting community commitment. For the community to fully support a program, they must be involved in the planning, the implementation, and the evaluation of the plan. To merely ask them to support what someone else is doing, irrespective of their input, is to invite almost certain disaster. School safety is all about partnerships and collaboration.

Involving parents

Next to students, parents are the most important resource in promoting safe schools and ensuring the success of their children. Their involvement in the planning process and their presence on campus is critical. Their presence in the school promotes quality education. Several model programs support this concept. Successful school administrators enlist more than parental support — they seek parental participation and involvement.

For example, when George McKenna served as the principal of Washington Preparatory High School in Los Angeles, his goal was to have at least 12 parents involved in the school's programs each day. Parents were recruited and assigned to visit classrooms, serve as guest lecturers, and help patrol hallways, restrooms, playgrounds, and the cafeteria. Their mere presence sent a message to students that school is important.

At John G. Osborne Elementary School in Houston, principal Gloria Jones orchestrated 100 percent parent involvement for many years running. Generally, her staff reached most parents through normal invitations and open houses. However, when parents refused to come to the school, Jones — a sort of educational evangelist — went to them in creative ways (see "Ten Commandments for Parents" on page 52). She personally followed up by making telephone calls and personal visits at places of work, worship, and community events. Granted, this type of commitment goes beyond the usual job expectation, but Jones believes that today's climate requires new approaches to reach parents and students alike. She worked with parents and conducted parent workshops on the role of parents in supporting their children.

About 700 Chicago parents have organized to eliminate gang recruitment at elementary schools by patrolling school grounds and the

Ten Commandments for Parents
(of which the 11th is the greatest)

1. Thou shalt have no other interest besides thy children.

2. Thou shalt not try to make thy children into an image of thyself, for they are individuals filled with curiosity and wonder, even though they constantly wiggle all the day long. They will show interest and will cooperate with those who will give them a fair amount of freedom while playing.

3. Thou shall not scream the names of thy children during irritating moments, for they will not hold thee in respect if thou screameth their name in vain.

4. Remember each Saturday and keep it happy.

5. Thou shalt not kill one breath of stirring endeavor in the heart of your child.

6. Honor the feelings of thy children, that their conduct in public may speak well of thee and thy household.

7. Thou shalt not suffer any unkindness of speech or action to enter the door of thy residence.

8. Thou shalt not steal for the drudgery of a "day's work" the precious hours that should be given to recreation, that thy love and understanding may appear unto all that come into thy household.

9. Thou shalt not bear witness to too many hours of indulging the idol called television, for thy brain may become weary and thy body obese.

10. Thou shalt not covet they neighbor's house, nor her children, nor her mannerisms, nor her ways of doing things, nor anything that is thy neighbor's. Work out thine own salvation with fear and trembling—only don't let anyone know about the fear and trembling.

11. Thou shalt laugh—when it rains and woolly-smelling wee ones muddy the floor, when the wind blows and the doors bang; when the little angels conceal their wings and wiggle, when Tommy spills milk and Mary drops your finest plate of china, when visitors appear at the precise moment that each child has forgotten everything you've ever taught them. And again, I say unto you — Laugh, for upon these commandments hang all the law and profits of the household.

—Paraphrased by Alfreda Jones
at the request of her daughter, Gloria Jones
April, 1984

neighboring community. The Chicago Intervention Network has conducted anti-gang classes at dozens of schools, to teach parents, students, and teachers about gang symbols and recruitment tactics. At the once gang-plagued Chopin School, parents patrol the grounds wearing orange armbands, keeping order, occasionally calling police, and driving gang members away.

In Seattle, Superintendent of Schools William Kendrick wants to match a parent or "surrogate somebody" with every student within the school district. He has recruited more than 11,000 parents, community members, and business leaders to serve as mentor role models for students.

Working with the media

Include the media as a vital safe schools team member. Remember that it is the school administrator's responsibility to project the type of image the school wants to portray. The absence of such a plan leaves the public message to chance.

When school crime information becomes available as a result of data collection efforts of the safe schools team, the media may produce public interest articles about the safety of campuses. Rather than supporting the school's sincere efforts to reduce violence, the articles sometimes damage a school's reputation by labeling a school as a source of "high" crime. When there is no mandated crime reporting, it is sometimes assumed there is no crime problem. On the other hand, when a school first decides to monitor school crime, the effect can be equally alarming. The media can help by keeping these influences of reporting and nonreporting in perspective.

One means of diffusing adverse publicity relies on the district's readiness with articles and information for the media. Such resources acknowledge safe schools' needs, describe strategies initiated to reduce the presence of crime and violence on the campus, and compare school crime and violence rates with those of the local community supplied by local law enforcement agencies. Without a proactive school crime publicity campaign, schools remain vulnerable to the media message. Adverse publicity also can tempt school officials to under-report the incidence of crime on their campuses to avoid negative labels. If this happens, the efforts of your safe schools planning team can be undermined.

Media strategies

School crime and violence incidents will attract the press. An important component of school district policies should involve the establishment of specific guidelines and expectations for working with the media. This would include:

- identifying a spokesperson
- providing appropriate space to the media for interviews
- having adequate crisis communications capability
- providing in-service training to individuals who will represent the district

The interviewee often feels as though he or she is at the mercy of the reporter. However, the interviewee has rights and should take control of the situation. There are several strategies that can be set in place. First, ask questions before speaking into the microphone — What is the nature of your interview? — Which direction are you going to take? — What do you already know about the situation? These are questions you should feel comfortable asking before the interview begins. Let the interviewer know what you are prepared to discuss. Don't sit down for the interview until you are ready. Avoid potential distractions. You have the right to be treated fairly. Be comfortable and look comfortable. Realize that the interview is not simply a discussion between you and the reporter, it is a communication with a wide listening or viewing audience.

There are several myths that should be dispelled when dealing with the media. They include:

Myth: The reporter determines the length of the interview.

Fact: The interviewee can set time parameters.

Myth: You can talk to a reporter "off the record."

Fact: Don't talk "off the record" unless you have updated your resume.

Myth: The interview starts when the reporter asks you the first question.

Fact: The interview starts when you first meet the reporter.

Myth: You are there to answer the reporter's questions.

Fact: You are there to tell the "real" story. Determine your objectives. You may use notes for facts, quotes, key words.

Myth: You must answer every question as it is asked.

Fact: If uncomfortable, ask that the question be repeated or rephrased. Develop your plan and know your objectives. If you cannot answer the question, you can say, "I can't answer that question." Never say, "No comment."

Myth: Your audience is the reporter.

Fact: Your real audience is the person reading the newspaper and watching the news. Use language the average person would understand.

Myth: I can wing the interview. After all, I am only being interviewed by the local reporter.

Fact: Most media outlets are connected to a national network. The local interview may have a national audience.

Myth: The reporter is in control of the interview.

Fact: You are the person being interviewed. Be proactive. Be prepared. You can set the tone and the pace.

Myth: I must talk if the reporter is silent.

Fact: Be alert to the waiting tactic. Most people can stand only 6.5 seconds of silence. Reporters know this. When you have said all you need to say— STOP!

Myth: The interview is over when the reporter says thank you for being interviewed or when you think the camera has stopped rolling.

Fact: The interview is not over until you are driving away from the studio or the reporter has left the school.

Chapter 7

Evaluating the Results

Every school should conduct an annual school safety assessment and review of their safe school plan. A school safety assessment is a strategic evaluation of the entire plan, including the associated policies, people, and processes that work together to make the plan happen.

Safe school planning is an ongoing process. In this sense, the evaluation component is a continuing reality check and refinement of the safe school actions and attitudes that the safe schools team wishes to create. The assessment may reveal that additional steps should be taken to improve adult supervision, revise curricula, pass legislation, redesign facilities, or establish new programs. Changes in the school budget may dictate that new or different programs be implemented.

The safe schools planning team and the community should be involved in the evaluation process on a regular basis. Emerging school safety issues, as well as each component of the safe school plan, should be examined to ascertain how they affect school climate, school attendance, personal safety, and overall school security. The safety assessment includes, but is not necessarily limited to:
- A review of student discipline policies, problems, procedures, and practices at both the school site and district level
- A review of the incident reporting system
- An evaluation of the school safety plan and planning process
- An assessment of the school/law enforcement partnership and the school's relationship with local community leaders and resources
- A review of crime prevention efforts with regard to environmental design
- A review of employee recruiting, selection, supervision and training criteria as they pertain to school safety
- An assessment of student activity and extra-curricular programs
- A review of the crisis prevention and response plan
- An assessment of the educational plan and its support for a positive school climate
- A review of other such areas deemed necessary by the evaluation of the district or site.

The important thing is to go back to your original safe school plan, review every component and ask the following questions:
- Is this priority on task?

- What could we do better?
- Do other options or strategies exist that we should try?
- How can we be more effective?
- How can we combine other efforts or strategies to produce better results?

For instance, if you are reviewing your school crime reporting plan, several questions should be incorporated into the assessment.

- Is there a district policy on school crime reporting?
- Are criminal activities clearly distinguished from disciplinary matters?
- Are standard forms used throughout the district?
- Are staff and students aware of state school-crime reporting laws?
- Are school safety laws being observed?
- Has someone been identified to coordinate the incident reporting system?
- Are incident reports reviewed in terms of crime analysis?
- Are regular summaries (monthly, quarterly, and annual crime reports) compiled?
- Is the public (including both parents and the press) regularly informed of the levels of school crime and violence?

At least once a year, review your mission statement to help you remain focused on your top priority of serving and preparing young people for productive and responsible citizenship. The bottom line is, an evaluation is never done. It should continue on a regular and continuing basis.

Appendix I includes a variety of self-assessment tools and questionnaires which will complement the evaluation process.

Chapter 8

Guidelines for Policy Development

Once a clear analysis of the top school safety and security issues has been developed within the district, existing policies regarding safe schools should be reviewed. It may be time to create a series of new school safety policies. These policies will shape and direct the administrative efforts to create a positive learning environment — free of violence, intimidation, and fear — where students can learn in a safe, welcoming, and drug- and alcohol-free climate.

The following violence prevention policy statement was adapted from *Violence in Schools,* published by the Virginia Association of School Superintendents:

It is the responsibility of schools and their governing authorities to provide safe schools for the children and communities that they serve. The establishment of safe schools is inseparable from the issues of violence and crime in the larger community. Safe school solutions must ultimately be pursued in the context of a commitment to create safe communities, not just safe schools. The broadest possible coordinated response of parents, educators, students, community leaders, and public and private agencies will be sought.

The developing right to safe schools includes the right of students and staff:
- To be protected against foreseeable criminal activity
- To be protected against student crime or violence which can be prevented by adequate supervision
- To be protected against identifiable dangerous students
- To be protected from dangerous individuals negligently admitted to school
- To be protected from dangerous individuals negligently placed in school
- To be protected from school administrators, teachers, and staff negligently selected, retained, or trained

Policies represent a guide for action. Good policies prevent problems before they occur and can help mitigate problems once they emerge. Good policies can also preclude a series of successive problems which might otherwise occur in the absence of appropriate policies. School districts and organizations tend to experience problems and management difficulties in those areas that lack appropriate policies and procedures. Without planning and policy development, anything can happen.

Well-designed policies tend to take the chance and risk out of school operations, establishing a standard for behavior and a common body of knowledge. They are simply a way to establish control and order on the school campus.

Policies should be written with several specific objectives in mind. They should:

- Support the educational mission of the district
- Serve as guidelines for action
- State the governing board's position
- Be written in general language that is easy to apply
- Identify the critical goals and standards
- Allow for some degree of interpretation and flexibility in their application
- Be clearly communicated, consistently enforced, and fairly applied
- Be developed at the board level with the input of those who will have to implement the policies
- Be reviewed on a regular basis

Policies, like safe school planning, reflect the will of the community. Policies set the stage for the district's educational and supervisory program. Policies answer these questions: What kind of behavior do we want to promote, and what kind of behavior do we wish to avoid? What results do we wish to achieve, and what problems do we wish to avoid? The most exciting aspect of policy planning and development is that it allows administrators, along with the community they serve, to cooperatively and collaboratively develop the program goals and standards by which the district will be managed and evaluated.

In a 1993 report titled *Violence in the Schools*, The National School Boards Association recommends that the following questions should be considered as school districts develop violence prevention policies:

- Is the content of the policy within the scope of the board's authority?
- Is it consistent with local, state, and federal laws?
- Have legal references been included?
- Does it reflect good educational practice?
- Is it reasonable? (Are any requirements or prohibitions arbitrary or discriminatory?)
- Does it adequately cover the issue?
- Is it limited to one policy topic?
- It is cross-referenced to other relevant policy topics?
- Is it consistent with the board's existing policies?
- Can it be administered?
- Is it practical in terms of administrative enforcement and budget?

At the foundation of violence prevention are well-written and communicated student discipline regulations. As student discipline regulations are developed, 10 basic rules should be followed:

1. All school districts should have student disciplinary rules.
2. Rules must conform to applicable statutes.
3. Rules must conform to constitutional requirements.
4. Rules must be reasonable and not oppressive.
5. Rules should be clear.
6. Adopt rules in good faith; do not design rules to serve some ulterior motive.
7. Rules must serve a public purpose and enable the school to perform its function.
8. Rules should be written in appropriate form.
9. Rules must be approved in the manner required by law by the governing authority.
10. Student disciplinary rules must be disseminated.

Board policies regarding drug prevention are also fundamental. According to the United States Department of Education, schools which are successful in providing drug-free learning environments share seven common characteristics. Board policies regarding drug prevention efforts within the district should reflect these success factors:

1. Successful schools recognize, assess, and monitor the student drug-use problem.
2. Interaction and networking with community groups and agencies are necessary.
3. Drug-free schools have set, implemented, and enforced their anti-drug policies.
4. Curriculum choices, selection of materials, and the actual teaching of the prevention curriculum are specific to each school and address the reasons why students succumb to substance use/abuse.
5. Administrators, teachers, and staff are trained to be positive role models for students.
6. Effective schools involve students in drug-free activities. It is not sufficient to teach avoidance; alternatives to drug use are required.
7. Parental involvement is encouraged, and parent education is provided.

School districts can exercise two specific policy options relative to drug and alcohol prevention. The first involves the establishment and enforcement of a drug-free school zone. It is important to develop a close relationship with local law enforcement officials. Invite them to be an integral part of the academic, social, and formal supervision program of the school.

Second, an effective drug-free school program can be supported by the implementation of nuisance abatement laws for drug and gang houses. In this regard, it will be important for school officials to work with local government officials in developing ordinances and codes which prevent and intervene in situations involving illegal drug use. Drug houses should not be tolerated in or around schools. An example of a sample nuisance abatement process is reprinted on pages 61 and 62.

It is essential to develop policies which establish crisis prevention, preparation, management, and resolution strategies. The crisis plan should include:

- Specific procedures for handling a crisis
- A clear chain of command
- A designated crisis command center
- A districtwide communications plan which specifies the equipment needed and the procedures for how it will be used
- Specifically assigned roles
- Crisis counseling

A comprehensive set of safe school policies should be developed which support the educational mission of the district. These policies may include, but are not necessarily limited to, the following areas:

- **Alternative activities for young people**
  Work opportunities
  Community service programs
  Extracurricular activities

- **Collaboration with other agencies**
  Interagency information/record sharing
  Collaborative development of probation conditions

- **Crime-free school zones**
  Drug-free school zones
  Gun-free school zones
  Weapon-free school zones
  Gang-free school zones
  Establishing "safe havens" for students

- **Student conduct/discipline code**
  Expulsion
  Suspension
  Alternative programs or schools
  Dress code
  Student photo ID system
  Closed campus for lunch

- **Emergency preparedness**

- **Home-school linkages**
  Parent skills training
  Volunteer parent patrols
- **Search and seizure issues**
  Camera surveillance/intrusion-control systems
  Metal detectors
  Locker searches
  Drug-detecting dogs
- **Security personnel in schools**
  Enhanced training for school peace officers
  School/law enforcement partnerships
- **Specialized curriculum and/or training**
  Conflict resolution/mediation training
  Law-related education programs
  Mentoring programs/support programs
  Multicultural sensitivity training
  Staff development
- **Weapons in school**
  Control campus access
  Create a weapons reporting hotline
  Establish zero-tolerance of weapons policies

Increase adult supervision
Metal detectors
Security improvements
Violence prevention curricula

Undoubtedly, school districts should also develop policy guidelines on student behavior, campus management, school design, emergency preparedness, and a host of other issues. However, the purpose of this planning and procedure guide is to have school planners begin and continue the thinking process that leads to safer and better schools.

A consultant could come in to a school district and write a comprehensive safe schools plan in a matter of two or three days. However, the plan, most likely, would not work because an effective safe school plan must be created, implemented, managed, and evaluated by those who are responsibile for its ongoing success. When this happens, communities have a better chance to create a successful — and safe — educational experience for all children and those individuals who serve them.

WANT TO CLOSE A DRUG
HOUSE ON YOUR BLOCK?
THE $4 SOLUTION

"We look at a drug house as a property management problem and drug use as anti-social, anti-moral behavior that creates a public nuisance," says Molly Wetzel of the Drug Abatement Institute (DAI) in Oakland, California. "If the property owner won't evict the drug dealers, then the neighbors go to small claims court and sue for damages for emotional and mental distress. And they win, every time."

In August 1989, 18 neighbors (including Wetzel) of a drug and prostitution-plagued apartment won $1,500 each, plus court costs, in a judgment against a landlord who had not responded to pleas to evict problem tenants. Calling itself Safe Streets Now!, this group shares the expertise gained from its precedent-setting case with people looking for nonviolent nonconfrontational ways to rid their communities of drug and gang houses. Safe Streets Now!, through the DAI, teaches others how to use California's state nuisance abatement laws — originally enacted to protect neighborhood peace and harmony — to sue in small claims court, which charges a $4 filing fee, prohibits lawyers, and guarantees a hearing in 30 days. Because a plaintiff can sue for up to $5,000, lawsuits filed by every family member in neighboring households seriously threaten a landlord's profits.

The DAI stresses that a drug house, like any other business, has staff, customers, deliveries, and sales. But its business destroys a neighborhood's quality of life through excessive noise day and night, increases in crime and violence, propositions and threats to residents, and litter including the health-threatening debris of used syringes and condoms. This public

nuisance forces children and adults to forsake the streets and hide in their homes.

Small Claims Court Process — Simple and Inexpensive in California

The small claims court route is nonconfrontational, simple, and "very empowering" to individuals, according to Molly Wetzel. First, concerned residents form a neighborhood team composed of neighbors, the beat police officer, and a city council representative. After identifying the property owner through city records, team members document the public nuisance impact of the drug house. They maintain activity logs on customers and deliveries, prostitution, and incidents of loud noise and fights. Involved residents call the police whenever they suspect drug trafficking or prostitution; they also phone neighbors who may have observed the same situation and ask them to document the activity and call the police. These reports lay a paper trail for use in court. Collecting data involves all ages. In one case, children playing jacks and skipping rope on the street counted the drug deals on one corner and went inside homes to record hourly totals. At no time does a neighbor or the team confront the drug dealer.

After gathering evidence, the neighborhood team — using a group name or the DAI to insure privacy — sends a letter to the rental unit's owner notifying him of the public nuisance. The owner also gets copies of activity logs and press clippings describing successful anti-nuisance lawsuits in small claims court. The letter offers the support of the neighborhood team and the police in any eviction efforts. If significant action is not taken within two weeks, the neighborhood team sues the property owner. A

Reprinted, with permission, from *The Catalyst* (May 1991).

hearing is scheduled within 30 days. Under this pressure, many landlords move rapidly to deal with problem tenants.

If a case does go to court, maps, activity logs, and bags of debris bring the drug house vividly into the courtroom. The group describes the business of drugs in their neighborhood and how they have "bent over backwards" to fight it. Claimants each take a few minutes to tell the judge how the drug house has changed their lives and the mental and emotional distress they have suffered.

After a successful lawsuit that closes a drug house, DAI works with owners, neighbors, and community agencies to help repair the property and clean up the streets. About half the drug house entrepreneurs move elsewhere, and half leave the business. DAI finds that many drug dealers who grew up in the neighborhood go into treatment or find another livelihood once collective community action has closed a drug house and re-established certain standards of conduct.

"Money Isn't the Issue"

DAI has helped close about 60 drug houses in California and trained more than 1,000 people there and in other states. "There's been no retaliation or threats," comments Wetzel. "It's the power of the people, and it's amazing." She also stresses the impact on neighborhood children. "Kids are transformed. They help collect evidence, and they testify. We don't realize how a drug house impacts children. They have no choice to be good, because they take their lives in their hands when walking to school or to the store. Closing a drug house gives them a choice. We also teach them to use the laws and introduce them to the police and the courts in a positive way."

Wetzel, now a member of Oakland's City Council, personalizes her fight against drugs when she recounts how her son was robbed of 55 cents at gunpoint and told her "there was nothing we could do against the drug dealers. He got involved with a gang, and our family was being torn apart. He turned around when we won our lawsuit and he saw that law abiding people could triumph. Some families have gotten as much as $6,000 in judgements, but money isn't the issue. It's a matter of taking back the neighborhood, making it clean and safe for families, and restoring a sense of village."

For more information, contact Molly Wetzel, Drug Abatement Institute, 1221 Broadway, Plaza Level, Suite 13, Oakland, CA 94612; 415/525-6587. ▼

Model Assessment Questionnaires

School Crime and Violence Incident Report Form 65
  Florida Department of Education
School Incident Report of Criminal Offenses.. 67
  South Carolina Department of Education
Incident Reporting Checklist.. 71
  South Carolina Department of Education
Model Safe Schools Checklist 73
  South Carolina Department of Education
Assessment Survey: Security Checklist 79
Emergency Preparedness Policy and Planning Checklist 83
Duty Personnel Assignment Checklist 85
School CPTED Survey: School Security Survey Form 87
Student School Safety Survey I 95
Student School Safety Survey II 97
Parent School Safety Survey.. 99
Teacher School Safety Survey 101
Teacher Discipline and Classroom Management Self-Assessment 103
Quality Management in the Classroom Checklist: Teacher Self-Assessment 105
Interview Questions for Security Officers... 107
Security Maintenance Checklist 109
Frequency of Security and Safety Maintenance Checklist 121
Risk Management Checklist 123
Weapons Checklist 125
Youth Gangs Checklist 127
Transportation Safety Checklist 129
Field Trip Checklist 131

Return for to your District Contact who will return it by August 12, 1994 to:

Consultant, School Crime and Violence
Florida Department of Education
Room 722, Florida Education Center
Tallahassee, Florida 32399-0400
(904) 487-2280, SunCom 277-2280

Florida Department of Education
Division of Public Schools
School Crime and Violence Incident Report Form

School Year 1993-94

District Name: _____   District Number: _____
School Name: _____   School Number: _____

Directions: All incidents resulting in either a disciplinary action, suspension, or expulsion should be included. Report only those incidents that are committed by students who are part of your district's responsibility. **ALWAYS REPORT THE PRESENCE OF ALCOHOL, DRUGS, OR WEAPONS OR WHETHER THE INCIDENT IS GANG-RELATED FOR ALL INCIDENTS.** That is, report the involvement of a weapon in an incident in both the incident category that is the primary category and also in the column for weapons. Similarly, report the presence of alcohol or narcotics along with the incident. If the incident of breaking and entering involves alcohol, report the incident in both the total incidents column for breaking and entering and the alcohol/drug related column for breaking and entering. If several actions occur in a single overall incident, report the most serious of the actions. For example, if the incident involves both fighting and battery, report the battery. See the instructions/examples on the back of the form for further definitions of the categories used for reporting. For all incidents, provide the number of the occurrences that resulted in a report to the police.

For the category of **DISORDERLY CONDUCT**, report only those incidents which seriously disrupt the orderly conduct of school functions. Minor classroom offenses should not be included in this category.

Type of Incident	Line No.	Total Incidents	Reported to Police	Gang Related	Alcohol/Drug Related	Firearms Involved	Other Weapons Involved
Alcohol (possession, use, or sale)	01				XXXXXXXXX		
Arson (setting a fire on or in school property)	02						
Assault (threat of physical harm)	03						
Battery (physical attack/harm)	04						
Breaking and Entering/Burglary (school building or vehicle)	05						
Disorderly Conduct (serious disruption)	06						
Fighting (mutual altercation)	07						
Firearm Incident/Possession	08					XXXXX	
Homicide (killed on campus)	09						
Larceny/Theft (personal or school property)	10						
Malicious Harassment/Hate Crimes	11						
Motor Vehicle Theft (including attempted)	12						
Narcotics Excluding Alcohol (illegal drug possession, use, or sale)	13				XXXXXXXXX XXXXXXXX		
Other Weapons Possession (other than firearms)	14						XXXXXXXXXXXXX
Robbery (using force)	15						
Sexual Battery (including attempted)	16						
Sexual Harassment	17						
Sex Offenses (lewd behavior/indecent behavior)	18						
Trespassing (school property or school function)	19						
Vandalism (destruction of school property)	20						
Other Major Crime/Violence (bomb threat, abduction, kidnapping, etc.)	21						

School Crime and Violence Incident Report Form
Definitions for Incident Reporting

All incidents resulting in a disciplinary action, suspension, or expulsion should be included in this report. Incidents occurring at school functions, at after school activities (even if off campus), and on school related and/or supported transportation should also be included. Any incident involving a firearm or other weapon should be included in the proper category AND in EITHER the **Firearms** or **Other Weapons** column. Any incident involving alcohol or narcotics should be included in the **Alcohol/Drug Related** Column.

Given below are the definitions to be used to report the incidents in this report. Questions regarding these definitions should be directed to your district contact.

Alcohol: The violation of laws or ordinances prohibiting the manufacture, sale, purchase, transportation, possession or use of intoxicating alcoholic beverages.

Arson: To unlawfully or intentionally damage, or attempt to damage, any real or personal property by fire or incendiary device.

Assault: Any intentional, unlawful threat, by word or act, to do violence to another person, coupled with an apparent ability to do so, and doing some act that creates a well-founded fear in another person that violence is imminent.

Battery: An actual and intentional touching or striking of another person against his or her will or intentionally causing bodily harm to an individual, including child abuse.

Breaking and Entering/Burglary: The unlawful entry into a building or other structure with the intent to commit a felony or theft.

Disorderly Conduct: Any act which **substantially** disrupts the orderly conduct of a school function, behavior which **substantially** disrupts the orderly learning environment or poses a threat to the health, safety, and/or welfare of students, staff, or others; repeated misconduct. If the action results in a more serious incident, report in the more serious incident category.

Fighting: Mutual participation in an altercation

Firearm Incident/Possession: Includes firearms of any kind (operable or inoperable, loaded or unloaded), including, but not limited to zip, pistol, rifle, shot gun, BB gun, starter gun, explosive propellant, or destructive device.

Homicide: Murder and non-negligent manslaughter, killing of one human being by another, killing a person through negligence.

Larceny/Theft: The unlawful taking, carrying, leading, or riding away of property from the possession, or constructive possession, of another person. Included are pocket picking, purse snatching, theft from a building, theft from a motor vehicle (except motor vehicle parts/accessories), theft of bicycles, theft from a machine or device which is operated or activated by the use of a coin or token and all other types.

Malicious Harassment/Hate Crimes: Intentionally intimidating or harassing another person because of that person's race, religion, color, sexual orientation, ancestry, or national origin.

Motor Vehicle Theft: The theft or attempted theft of a motor vehicle.

Narcotics, Excluding Alcohol: The unlawful use, cultivation, manufacture, distribution, sale, purchase, possession, transportation, or importation of any controlled drug or narcotic substance, or equipment and devices used for preparing or taking drugs or narcotics.

Other Weapons Possession: Any instrument or object deliberately used to inflict harm on another person, or used to intimidate any person. Included in this category are knives of any kind, chains (any not being used for the purpose for which it was normally intended and capable of harming an individual), pipe (any length, metal or otherwise, not being used for the purpose for which it was intended), razor blades or similar kinds of instruments, ice picks, dirks, or other pointed instruments (including pencils and pens), nunchakas, brass knuckles, Chinese stars, billy clubs, tear gas guns, or electrical weapons or devices (stun guns).

Robbery: The taking or attempting to take anything of value under confrontation circumstances from the control, custody, or care of another person by force or threat of force or violence and/or putting the victim in fear of larcenies.

Sexual Battery: Any sexual act or attempt directed against another person, forcibly and/or against the person's will where the victim is incapable of giving consent because of his or her youth or because of temporary or permanent mental incapacity. This category includes rape, touching of private body parts of another person (either through human contact or using an object), indecent liberties, child molestation, and sodomy.

Sexual Harassment: Sexual harassment includes any of the following actions or activities:

1. Any slur, innuendo, or other verbal or physical conduct reflecting on an individual's gender which has the purpose or effect of creating an intimidating, hostile, or offensive educational or work environment; has the purpose or effect of unreasonably interfering with an individual's work or school performance or participation; or otherwise affects an individual's employment or educational opportunities.

2. The denial of or provision of aid, benefits, grades, rewards, employment, faculty assistance, services, or treatment on the basis of sexual advances or requests for sexual favors.

3. Sexual advances, requests for sexual favors, and other verbal or physical conduct of a sexual nature when submission to such conduct is made either explicitly or implicitly a term or condition of an individual's employment or educational career; submission to or rejection of such conduct is used as a basis for educational or employment decisions affecting the individual; or such conduct has the purpose or effect of unreasonably interfering with an individual's work or educational performance or creating an intimidating, hostile or offensive working or educational environment.

Sex Offenses: This is unlawful sexual intercourse, sexual contact or other unlawful behavior or conduct intended to result in sexual gratification without force or threat and where the victim is capable of giving consent. Included in this category are indecent exposure (exposure of private body parts to the sight of another person in a lewd or indecent manner in a public place), and obscenity (conduct by which the community standards is deemed to corrupt public morals by its indecency and/or lewdness such as phone calls or other communication; unlawful manufacture, publishing, selling, buying, or possessing materials such as literature or photographs).

Trespassing: To enter or remain on a public school campus or school board facility or event without authorization, invitation and with no lawful purpose for entry, including students under suspension or expulsion, employees not required by their employment to be at the particular location; and unauthorized persons who enter or remain on campus or school board facility or sponsored activity after being directed to leave by the chief administrator or designee of the facility, campus, or function.

Vandalism: The willful and/or malicious destruction, damage, or defacement of public or private property, real or personal, without the consent of the owner or the person having custody or control of it. This category includes graffiti.

Other Major Crime/Violence: Any major incident resulting in a disciplinary action such as a bomb threat, bribery, fraud, embezzlement, gambling or other action not included in any of the above incident categories.

ESE   741

School Incident Report of Criminal Offenses
South Carolina Department of Education

Reporting Requirement: This collection is mandated by the Safe Schools Act of 1990 (Act 579) which calls for the development of a standard crime report to be used throughout the State. Only criminal incidents which are committed on public school campuses; in travel to and from schools on public school buses; during public school functions; and involving public school students, employees, or property should be reported.

Instructions: (1) This report should be completed immediately after an incident of a criminal nature. Not all information will be available, but missing data may be filled in later or before the quarterly reporting is due. If the local law enforcement authority is called to investigate an incident, some of the requested information needed for this collection may be obtained from this agency's Incident Report. (2) A copy of all completed report(s) must be sent to your District Superintendent immediately after the end of a quarter. If no criminal offenses occurred during a reporting quarter, check here _____, circle the reporting quarter, complete the school identifiers and name of report completer, sign at the bottom of the reverse side of this page, and transmit the report to the District Superintendent. The District Superintendent will forward quarterly summary reports for the school district to the State Department of Education. Please refer to the instruction booklet for further information.

Reporting Quarter: Please circle the number which represents the quarter for which you are reporting:

1. Quarter 1 (Jun 1 - Aug 31)   2. Quarter 2 (Sep 1 - Nov 30)   3. Quarter 3 (Dec 1 - Feb 29)   4. Quarter 4 (Mar 1 - May 31)

Name of School:

_____

School Beds ID:

_____

Name of Report Completer:

_____

Offenses Occurring during this Incident (Check all that apply.)

_____ Aggravated Assault

_____ Arson

_____ Bribery

_____ Burglary/Breaking and Entering

_____ Counterfeiting/Forgery

_____ Disturbing Schools

Drug/Narcotic Offenses

    _____ Possession, Manufacture, etc.

    _____ Drug Equipment Violations

_____ Embezzlement

_____ Extortion/Blackmail

_____ Fraud Offenses

_____ Gambling Offenses

_____ Homicide

    _____ Murder

    _____ Negligent Manslaughter

    _____ Justifiable Homicide

_____ Kidnapping/Abduction

_____ Larceny/Theft Offenses

_____ Liquor Law Violations

_____ Motor Vehicle Theft

_____ Pornography/Obscene Material

_____ Prostitution

_____ Robbery

_____ Sex Offense, Forcible

_____ Sex Offense, Nonforcible

_____ Stolen Property Offense

_____ Threatening School
    Official or Family

_____ Vandalism/Destruction,
    Damage of Property

_____ Weapons Offense

_____ Other Offenses
(Specify)_____

Date Incident Occurred: _____

Time Incident Occurred:

_____ During School Day

_____ Before School (6 - 8 am)

_____ After School (3 - 6 pm)

_____ School Night (6 pm - 6 am)

_____ Weekend

_____ Vacation/Holiday

Where Incident Occurred (Check all that apply.)

_____ Athletic Field or Playground

_____ Cafeteria

_____ Classroom

_____ Gym or Locker Room

_____ Hallway or Stairs

_____ Storage Area

_____ On School Bus

_____ Restroom

_____ School Parking Lot

_____ School Yard

_____ Other (Specify) _____

_____

Perpetrator(s)/Offender(s) Descriptive Information:

If the perpetrator(s) is (are) unknown, check here _____; otherwise, enter the number of perpetrators in each category. (Be sure to supply an age for each perpetrator even if the age is the same for more than one perpetrator.)

Gender: Male _____   Female _____   How many perpetrators were special education students? _____

Age(s) of the Perpetrator(s): _____

The Perpetrator(s) is (are): (Indicate number in each category)

_____ A student at this school   _____ Parent/Guardian   _____ A student on suspension or expulsion from
_____ A student at another school   _____ A student on suspension   school at the time of the incident
_____ An employee at this school   or expulsion from another   _____ Other (specify) _____
      (Specify job title) _____   school at the time of the   _____
      _____   incident

Victim(s) Descriptive Information

If there is no victim, check here _____; otherwise, enter the number of victims in each category. (Be sure to supply an age for each victim even if the age is the same for more than one victim.)

Gender: Male _____   Female _____   How many victims were special education students? _____

Age(s) of Victim(s): _____

The Victim(s) is (are): (Indicate number in each category)

_____ A student at this school   _____ Parent/Guardian   _____ A student on suspension or expulsion from
_____ A student at another school   _____ A student on suspension   school at the time of the incident
_____ An employee at this school   or expulsion from another   _____ Other (specify) _____
      (Specify job title) _____   school at the time of the   _____
      _____   incident

Relationship/Circumstance

If no victim was involved in this incident, check here _____.

Were the victim(s) and perpetrator(s) known to each other?   _____ Yes   _____ No   _____ Don't Know

If yes, indicate the primary relationship.

_____ Victim/Perpetrator live in same neighborhood   _____ Victim/Perpetrator are relatives
_____ Victim/Perpetrator involved together in a business/illegal activity _____ Victim/Perpetrator romantically involved
_____ Victim/Perpetrator involved in same gang   _____ Victim/Perpetrator involved in different
_____ Other (Specify)_____   gangs

Weapon

What, if any, weapon(s) was (were) involved in the incident? (Check all that apply.)

_____ No weapon involved   _____ Other firearm   _____ Rope/chain, etc.
_____ Blunt object   _____ Hands/feet, etc.   _____ Other (Specify) _____
_____ Explosive   _____ Knife or other sharp object _____
_____ Handgun   _____ Metal knuckles

Cost

Please approximate the cost of the crime to the victim and/or the school. (These costs would include hospitalization or emergency room costs in the event of bodily injury, replacement costs of stolen or vandalized items or property, etc.) Exclude long-term costs such as trauma counseling.

Cost to Victim

_____ No Cost
_____ $1 - $99
_____ $100 - $499
_____ $500 - $999
_____ Over $1,000 please specify $_____
_____ Unknown

Cost to School

_____ No Cost
_____ $1 - $99
_____ $100 - $499
_____ $500 - $999
_____ Over $1,000 please specify $_____
_____ Unknown

Action Taken by the School Administration as a Result of this Incident (Check all that apply.)

_____ Notified local law enforcement agency
_____ Notified district security personnel
_____ Notified local fire marshal
_____ Began suspension or expulsion procedure
_____ Other (specify)_____
_____

_____ Improved school security procedures
_____ Made available counseling at school
_____ Recommended professional counseling (hospital/clinic)
_____ Made use of hospital facilities for injuries

Certification

I certify that the information contained in this incident report is true and correct to the best of my knowledge.

_____
Signature of the Principal or Designee

Incident Reporting Checklist*
South Carolina Department of Education

Purpose: This incident reporting checklist itemizes elements that should be considered when establishing an incident reporting system at a school.

Directions: Check the line that best represents the current status of your incident reporting information. Use this information as input into your school's discussion on developing the reporting system and prioritizing needs for school improvement.

	Yes	No	In Process
1. An incident reporting procedure has been established for all criminal and violent incidents which take place on or near school property, at school-sponsored events, or on school-sponsored transportation.	—	—	—
2. The reporting procedure includes clear definitions of incidents and a set procedure for reporting, including who completes reports and how often these are submitted to school administrators.	—	—	—
3. Those responsible for reporting incidents are trained in definitions of incidents and reporting procedures.	—	—	—
4. Accident reports are filed when a student is injured on school property, at a school event, or on school-sponsored transportation.	—	—	—
5. A database is developed from the incident reports and it is used to identify recurring school safety problems and to plan for future school safety strategies.	—	—	—
6. Agreements have been made between local law enforcement and school administrators for the reporting of criminal and violent incidents to police.	—	—	—
7. If the school has a resource officer, agreements have been made between the officer and school administrators about incident reporting and information sharing.	—	—	—
8. Agreements between the school and law enforcement have been made on information-sharing on arrests and school incidents.	—	—	—
9. Agreements between the school and law enforcement have been made on the types of incidents in which law enforcement assistance will be necessary.	—	—	—

10. Those involved in reporting incidents are trained/updated every _____.
11. The incident reporting system is reviewed and updated every _____.
12. Incident reports and trends in incidents are analyzed every _____.

---

* Questions 1, 8, and 9 are adapted from the *School Safety Checklist*, South Carolina Department of Education, December 1990.

MODEL SAFE SCHOOLS CHECKLIST

APPROVED BY THE STATE BOARD OF EDUCATION
APRIL 10, 1991

Barbara S. Nielsen, Ed.D.
State Superintendent of Education

Office of School District Accreditation and Assessment
South Carolina Department of Education
Columbia, South Carolina

Purpose

The Model Safe Schools Checklist has been developed in compliance with Section 59-5-65 of the 1976 Code as amended by the General Assembly in 1990, pursuant to Regulation 43-166 adopted by the State Board of Education.

This model checklist is provided for use by school districts, or as a possible guide for developing a local checklist, to assist districts in assessing schools' safety strengths and weaknesses as required by state law.

This document is provided for guidance and assessment purposes only and is not intended to establish standards of preparedness or levels of safety to be met by all school districts.

The State Department of Education acknowledges with grateful appreciation the assistance provided by the National School Safety Center in preparation of this checklist.

Model Safe Schools Checklist

	Yes	No	NA
A. The existence of a comprehensive safety plan			
1. An emergency preparedness plan has been developed to address the following emergencies:			
a. Fire	___	___	___
b. Tornado	___	___	___
c. Hurricane	___	___	___
d. Bomb Threat/Explosion	___	___	___
e. School Bus Accident	___	___	___
f. Intruder	___	___	___
g. Earthquake	___	___	___
2. Threats unique to the school (e.g., nuclear accident, hazardous chemical release, train derailment) have been identified and the emergency preparedness plan addresses them.	___	___	___
a. _____	___	___	___
b. _____	___	___	___
c. _____	___	___	___
B. Communication of Discipline Policies and Procedures			
1. Students are made aware of behavioral expectations and school discipline procedures.	___	___	___
2. Parents are made aware of and acknowledge student behavioral expectations and school discipline procedures.	___	___	___
C. Intra-Agency and Interagency Emergency Planning			
1. School emergency plans are coordinated with district emergency plans.	___	___	___
2. School emergency plans have been developed in cooperation with law enforcement and other emergency response agencies.	___	___	___
D. Recording of Disruptive Incidents			
1. Violations of state and federal law that occur on school grounds are reported immediately by school officials to the appropriate law enforcement agencies.	___	___	___
2. An incident reporting procedure has been established for all disruptive incidents which take place on school property.	___	___	___
3. A database is developed from disruptive incident reports, and it is analyzed to identify recurring school safety problems.	___	___	___

	Yes	No	NA

E. Training of Staff and Students

1. Training sessions and drills are conducted on a regular basis to test the effectiveness and efficiency of safety plans and procedures.

2. Parents, students, teachers, and administrators are involved in reviewing school policies and prevention strategies involved in school safety.

3. Staff training is provided in weapons detection and reporting, and in responding to confrontations when weapons are involved.

4. Staff training is provided to clarify expectations for reporting and responding to student violence.

5. Some staff members are trained in first aid and cardiopulmonary resuscitation (CPR).

6. Staff members are trained by law enforcement or other knowledgeable persons in the interception of and response to intruders.

F. Assessment of Building and Grounds

1. External doors are kept locked where feasible during school hours.

2. The capability exists to notify all teachers to lock classroom doors in an emergency.

3. School grounds are properly lighted for night activities.

4. The capability exists to monitor the main entrance.

5. Entrance doors have see-through safety glass.

6. All areas within the building are adequately lighted.

7. Student locker areas can be monitored by school staff.

8. Handrails are provided on stairways.

9. Steps are covered with a non-slip material.

10. Access to electrical panels in all areas is restricted.

11. Mechanical rooms and other hazardous material storage areas are kept locked.

12. Shrubbery and trees permit good visual surveillance of all parts of the school campus.

13. If feasible and potentially effective, the perimeter of the school is fenced in high traffic areas.

14. Visitor parking is clearly marked in a high visibility location as close to the main office as is feasible.

15. A high visibility area has been designated as the pickup/drop-off point for students and staff.

	Yes	No	NA

16. Access to bus loading areas by other vehicles is restricted where feasible. ___ ___ ___

17. Parking areas can be monitored by school staff. ___ ___ ___

18. Entrances and exits for parking areas are restricted to a minimum number. ___ ___ ___

G. Procedures for Handling Visitors

1. Visitors are required to report to the office. ___ ___ ___

2. A school policy for interception and response to unauthorized persons on campus is established. ___ ___ ___

3. Signs concerning visitor policy and trespassing are properly displayed at entrances to the campus and buildings. ___ ___ ___

H. Assignment of Personnel in Emergencies

1. An emergency team has been organized to carry out emergency plans and, if necessary, coordinate post-emergency activities with an external crisis intervention team. ___ ___ ___

2. Staff members have been assigned responsibilities to implement all parts of emergency plans. ___ ___ ___

3. An individual is designated to be responsible for overall school security procedures. ___ ___ ___

I. Emergency Communication and Management Procedures

1. The school has emergency telephone capability. ___ ___ ___

2. A procedure has been developed to notify bus drivers when emergency evacuation of buildings and grounds is necessary. ___ ___ ___

3. In the event of power failure, alarm systems and phones remain operative. ___ ___ ___

4. A communication capability between the office and all teaching stations exists. ___ ___ ___

J. Transportation Rules and Accident Procedures

1. School bus safety rules have been developed and distributed to all students. ___ ___ ___

2. Parents have been informed in writing of school bus safety rules. ___ ___ ___

3. All students participate in school bus emergency evacuation drills twice yearly. ___ ___ ___

4. Safety training is provided for all school bus drivers. ___ ___ ___

5. Drivers are trained in school bus discipline policies and procedures. ___ ___ ___

6. Accident procedures have been developed and communicated to bus drivers. ___ ___ ___

	Yes	No	NA

7. Passenger lists for all bus routes are maintained at the school site and are updated as changes occur. ___ ___ ___

8. Route descriptions for field trips are filed in the school office before trips begin. ___ ___ ___

9. Passenger lists are developed and filed in the school office for each vehicle going on a field trip. ___ ___ ___

10. All students and staff participating in a field trip carry identification with them. ___ ___ ___

11. Students with medical problems have identification of these problems on them when participating in field trips, or adult supervisors have a written listing of these medical problems. ___ ___ ___

Assessment Survey
Security Checklist

Give your school a thorough crime prevention inspection now. Use this checklist as a guideline to determine your school's strengths and weaknesses.

Organization   **Yes**   **No**

1. Is there a policy for dealing with violence and vandalism in your school? (The reporting policy must be realistic and strictly adhered to.) ___   ___
2. Is there an incident reporting system? ___   ___
3. Is the incident reporting system available to all staff? ___   ___
4. Is there statistical information available as to the scope of the problems at your school and in the community? ___   ___
5. Have the school, school board, and administrators taken steps or anticipated any problems through dialogue? ___   ___
6. Does security fit into the organization of the school? (Security must be designed to fit the needs of the administration and made part of the site.) ___   ___
7. Are the teachers and administrators aware of laws that pertain to them? To their rights? To students' rights? Of their responsibility as to the enforcement of and respect for rules, regulations, policies, and the law? ___   ___
8. Is there a working relationship with your local law enforcement agency? ___   ___
9. Are students aware of expectations and school discipline codes? Are parents aware? ___   ___
10. Are there any actual or contingency action plans developed to deal with student disruptions and vandalism? ___   ___
11. Is there a policy as to restitution or prosecution of perpetrators of violence and vandalism? ___   ___
12. Is there any in-service training available for teachers and staff in the areas of violence and vandalism and other required reporting procedures? ___   ___
13. Is there a policy for consistent monitoring and evaluation of incident reports? ___   ___
14. Is the staff trained in standard crime prevention behavior? ___   ___

Existing security system

1. Have there been any security problems in the past? ___   ___
2. Are there specific staff assigned or trained in security awareness? ___   ___
3. Is there an existing alarm system? ___   ___
4. Do you have intrusion-detection equipment? Have you consulted with an expert? ___   ___
5. If you have an alarm system, do you as an administrator know its capabilities and limitations? Do teachers and staff understand the basic working of the alarm system, so as to prevent leaving the security areas in such a condition as to cause needless false alarms? ___   ___

6. Do you have an alarm response policy and does everyone involved clearly understand their responsibilities? ___ ___
7. Is the system centrally located? ___ ___
8. Is it local? ___ ___
9. Is it a police alarm? ___ ___
10. Is there a policy for consistent maintenance and testing of the system? ___ ___
11. Do some members of the custodial staff work nights and weekends? ___ ___
12. Are valuable items of property identified? ___ ___
13. Are valuables properly stored? ___ ___
14. Are high-target areas properly secured? ___ ___
15. Is there a visitor procedure? ___ ___
16. Do students have I.D. cards or other identification? ___ ___
17. Do all employees have I.D. cards? ___ ___
18. Is there a policy for intruders, those who loiter, or non-students on campus? (To ensure a safe campus, violators should be arrested.) ___ ___
19. Is there proper visibility of parking areas? ___ ___
20. Is there supervision in hallways, corridors, and other congregating places for students between classes, at lunch, and before and after school? (Teachers and staff must participate in supervision.) ___ ___
21. Is the school designed with crime prevention in mind (landscaping, fencing, parking, and exterior lighting)? ___ ___
22. Is there a light/no-light policy for after-school hours? ___ ___
23. Whenever possible, is vandal damage repaired immediately? ___ ___

Target hardening/perimeter
1. Is there proper fencing around adjacent areas and target areas? ___ ___
2. Are gates properly secured with working locks? ___ ___
3. Is the perimeter free of rocks or gravel? ___ ___
4. Are signs properly posted as to rules and enforcement? ___ ___
5. Are signs properly designed for crime prevention? ___ ___
6. If there is exterior lighting, is it properly directed? Is there proper intensity? Are target areas well-lighted? Are there shadows? ___ ___
7. Are all grips, window ledges, roof accesses, and other equipment that could be used for climbing properly secured? ___ ___
8. Are all items removed from the building area that could be used to break in or stand and climb on? (Examples: lumber, ladders). ___ ___
9. Is the school designed for vandal-resistant walls? ___ ___
10. Do the school's texture, color, etc., act to deter vandal activity? ___ ___

Target hardening/exterior
1. Is there a key control system? ___ ___
2. Have outside handles been removed from doors that are used primarily as exits? ___ ___

	Yes	No

3. Are first-floor windows nonexistent or properly secured? ___ ___

4. Is broken window glass replaced with Plexiglas or other break-resistant material? ___ ___

5. Are school facilities kept neat and in good repair? ___ ___

6. Are school facilities sectioned off to limit access by evening users? ___ ___

7. Is after-hours use of playground facilities consistently and closely monitored? ___ ___

8. Are protective screens or window guards used? ___ ___

9. Can any door locks be reached by breaking out glass? ___ ___

10. Are your locks in good condition? ___ ___

11. Are doors equipped with security locks in mind? ___ ___

12. Are all exit doors secured by either deadbolts or chains and locks that will limit easy escape of vandals and/or burglars? ___ ___

13. Are locks maintained regularly and changed when necessary? ___ ___

14. Are doors constructed properly? ___ ___

15. Are door frames pry-proof? ___ ___

16. Are high-target areas (such as the shop, administrative offices, etc.) sufficiently secured? ___ ___

Target hardening/interior

1. Is school property permanently and distinctly marked? ___ ___

2. Has an inventory been made recently of school property? ___ ___

3. Are school files locked in vandal-proof containers? ___ ___

4. Are valuable items thieves can easily fence (such as typewriters, calculators, etc.) properly locked up or secured when not in use? (Valuable items should be stored in a security room or bolted down.) ___ ___

5. Is all money removed from cash registers? ___ ___

6. Are cabinets properly secured? ___ ___

Security system

1. Are there specific persons designated to secure buildings following after-hours activity? ___ ___

2. Is someone made responsible for overall school security procedures? ___ ___

3. Do job descriptions include vandalism prevention duties? ___ ___

4. Are security checklists used by school employees? ___ ___

5. Through as many channels as possible, are vandalism costs made known to taxpayers? ___ ___

6. Do local law enforcement agencies help and advise on vandalism prevention? ___ ___

7. Are administrators, teachers, and students urged to cooperate with police? ___ ___

8. Is evening and weekend use of school facilities encouraged? ___ ___

9. Do law enforcement or security personnel monitor school facilities during school hours? ___ ___

	Yes	No

10. Do law enforcement personnel, parents, or students patrol the grounds after school hours? ___ ___

11. Are local residents encouraged to report suspicious activity to school officials or police? ___ ___

12. Do students actively get involved in security efforts? ___ ___

13. Are there emergency procedures for incidents, including fire and bombing? ___ ___

Alarms

1. Is the entire system checked regularly or at least every six months? ___ ___

2. Is the number of false alarms kept down to below two for any six-month period? ___ ___

3. Can selected areas of the school be "zoned" by an alarm system that will indicate which area is being entered by the intruder? ___ ___

4. If public utility power fails, is there back-up power to keep the system operating without generating an alarm signal? ___ ___

5. Are suitable procedures established for response and turning on and off the alarm system? ___ ___

6. Are the alarms the self-resetting type? ___ ___

Modified from *The School Safety Checkbook*, © National School Safety Center, 1990. Original Source: *School Security: Get a Handle on a Vandal*, Sacramento, CA: California Department of Justice, School Safety Center, 1981.

Emergency Preparedness Policy and Planning Checklist*

Purpose: The Emergency Preparedness Policy and Planning Checklist contains items critical to ensuring general safety and school safety during times of emergency.

Directions: Check the line that best represents the current status of the school's emergency preparedness. Use this information as input into the school's discussion on prioritizing needs for school improvement.

1. An emergency preparedness plan has been developed in cooperation with law enforcement and emergency agencies for the following emergencies:

	Yes	No	In Process
a. Fire	___	___	___
b. Tornado	___	___	___
c. Hurricane	___	___	___
d. Bomb Threat/Explosion	___	___	___
e. School Bus Accident	___	___	___
f. Armed Individual	___	___	___
g. Abduction	___	___	___
h. Shooting on Campus	___	___	___

2. Threats unique to the school (nuclear accident, hazardous chemical release, etc.) have been identified and emergency preparedness plans have been developed for each (please list):

	Yes	No	In Process
_____	___	___	___
_____	___	___	___
_____	___	___	___

3. An emergency team has been organized to carry out emergency plans and, if necessary, coordinate post-emergency activities with an external crisis intervention team.   ___   ___   ___

4. Staff members have been assigned responsibilities to implement all parts of emergency plans.   ___   ___   ___

5. Substitutes have been designated for key members of the emergency team to ensure continued operation of emergency plans in the absence of any member of the team.   ___   ___   ___

---

* Questions 1–9, 11, & 13 are from the *School Safety Checklist*, South Carolina Department of Education, December 1990, p. 1–2.

	Yes	No	In process

6. Training sessions and drills are conducted on a regular basis to test the effectiveness and efficiency of various plans, procedures, and condition of equipment. ___ ___ ___

7. Facility "safe zones" have been identified for student and staff during crises such as tornado, hurricane, etc. ___ ___ ___

8. Contingency plans have been developed for complete evacuation of buildings and relocation of students and staff. ___ ___ ___

9. Contingency plans for evacuation of buildings and grounds include a plan for notifying bus drivers of the need for transportation. ___ ___ ___

10. Post-crisis/emergency follow-up plans have been developed and include all pertinent outside agencies. ___ ___ ___

11. A well-stocked first-aid kit is available in case of an emergency. ___ ___ ___

12. Selected staff members are trained in first aid and CPR. ___ ___ ___

13. The school has an unlisted telephone line to be used in an emergency.

___ ___ ___

14. Emergency preparedness plans are updated every _____.

15. Contingency plans are updated every _____.

16. Post-crisis plans are updated every_____.

17. Staff are trained in emergency plans and responsibilities every _____
_____.

18. Drills are conducted to test/practice plans and procedures every _____
_____.

Duty Personnel Assignment Checklist*

Purpose: The Duty Personnel Assignment Checklist serves to identify areas of the school considered to be critical in monitoring student safety.

Directions: Circle the answer that best represents the current status of duty personnel assignments at your school. Use this information as input into the school's staff discussion of issues requiring implementation or improvement.

1. Duty personnel have been assigned in the following critical school areas:

   a. Main entrance during all hours of operation.
       Yes   No

   b. Cafeteria during all lunch periods.
       Yes   No

   c. Bus pickup and drop-off points.
       Yes   No

	Student arrival		Between classes		Student departure		Lunch	
d. Stairways:	Yes	No	Yes	No	Yes	No	Yes	No
e. Locker clusters:	Yes	No	Yes	No	Yes	No	Yes	No
f. Restrooms:	Yes	No	Yes	No	Yes	No	Yes	No
g. Courtyards/ commons:	Yes	No	Yes	No	Yes	No	Yes	No
h. Student parking areas:	Yes	No	Yes	No	Yes	No	Yes	No
i. Corridors:	Yes	No	Yes	No	Yes	No	Yes	No

2. Monitoring duties are reviewed and/or reassigned every:
   6 months   1 year   2 years   Other_____

3. Monitoring duties/expectations are reviewed with duty personnel every:
   6 months   1 year   2 years   Other_____

4. Monitors are trained to deal with potential safety problems every:
   6 months   1 year   2 years   Other_____

*Question 1 (a–b, d–i) is adapted from the *School Safety Checklist*, South Carolina Department of Education, December 1990, p. 3.

School CPTED Survey
School Security Survey Form

A crime prevention through environmental design assessment attempts to evaluate the physical setting of facility and maintenance factors that affect the safety and crime quotient capability of a particular school. Environmental factors such as the types of neighborhoods, housing facilities, businesses, streets, and institutions surrounding the school affect the school's operation. Classrooms, security systems, lighting and color design, accessibility, and quality of maintenance are all evaluated to determine their effect upon school climate, natural supervision, defensible space, and differentiated space. The survey items are to be rated as satisfactory (S), unsatisfactory (U), or not applicable (NA).

I. **School Data**
   A. School _____

   B. School number _____

   C. Surveyed by _____

   D. Date _____

   E. School level _____
      1. High school _____
      2. Junior high _____
      3. Elementary _____
      4. Vocational _____
      5. Other _____

   F. Student population _____

   G. Premise type
      1. Single story _____
      2. Multiple story _____
      3. Enclosed design _____
      4. Tropical (open) _____
      5. Fortress _____
      6. Other _____

   H. Hours _____

II. **Neighborhood Area**
   A. Neighborhood type
      1. Commercial _____
      2. Industrial _____
      3. Residential _____
      4. Other _____

B. Housing
 1. Single _____
 2. Multiple _____
 3. High rise _____
 4. Low rise _____
 5. Public _____
 6. Other _____

C. Businesses
 1. Fast food _____
 2. Multiple _____
 3. High rise _____
 4. Low rise _____
 5. Other _____

D. Streets
 1. Major arterial(s) _____
 2. Business _____
 3. Residential _____
 4. Mixed _____
 5. Two-lane _____
 6. Four-lane _____
 7. Signals _____
 8. Other _____

E. Institutions
 1. Church(es) _____
 2. Schools
      Public _____
      Private _____
 3. Social club _____
 4. Hospital _____
 5. Recreational _____
 6. Other _____

F. Police reporting area _____

G. Comments _____
 _____

III. Interview Comments (Principal or Designer)
A. Problems
 1. _____
 2. _____
 3. _____
 4. _____

B. Needs
   1. _____
   2. _____
   3. _____
   4. _____

IV. Survey Items
A. Neighborhood
   1. Contact   S_____ U_____ NA_____
   2. Businesses   S_____ U_____ NA_____
   3. Traffic flows   S_____ U_____ NA_____
   4. Social   S_____ U_____ NA_____
   5. Other _____ S_____ U_____ NA_____
   6. Comments _____
   _____

B. School grounds border definition
   1. Fences   S_____ U_____ NA_____
   2. Foliage/trees   S_____ U_____ NA_____
   3. Gathering areas   S_____ U_____ NA_____
      Informal   S_____ U_____ NA_____
      Formal   S_____ U_____ NA_____
   4. Bus (loading zones) S_____ U_____ NA_____
   5. Police access   S_____ U_____ NA_____
   6. Furniture/amenities S_____ U_____ NA_____
   7. Other _____ S_____ U_____ NA_____
   8. Comments _____
   _____

C. Teachers' parking lot(s):
   1. Street(s)
      Access   S_____ U_____ NA_____
      Surveillance   S_____ U_____ NA_____
   2. Building(s)
      Access   S_____ U_____ NA_____
      Surveillance   S_____ U_____ NA_____

   3. Conflict with
      Bus zone   S_____ U_____ NA_____
      Gathering areas   S_____ U_____ NA_____
      Rec./DE   S_____ U_____ NA_____
      Other   S_____ U_____ NA_____
   4. Comments _____
   _____

D. Students' parking lot(s):
   1. Street(s)
      Access   S_____   U_____   NA_____
      Surveillance   S_____   U_____   NA_____
   2. Building(s)
      Access   S_____   U_____   NA_____
      Surveillance   S_____   U_____   NA_____
   3. Conflict with
        Bus zone   S_____   U_____   NA_____
        Gathering areas   S_____   U_____   NA_____
        Rec./DE   S_____   U_____   NA_____
        Other _____   S_____   U_____   NA_____
   4. Comments _____
        _____

E. Building(s)   *Access*
   1. Roof   S_____   U_____   NA_____
   2. Windows   S_____   U_____   NA_____
   3. Entrances   S_____   U_____   NA_____
   4. Comments _____
        _____

                                       Surveillance
   1. Roof   S_____   U_____   NA_____
   2. Windows   S_____   U_____   NA_____
   3. Entrances   S_____   U_____   NA_____

F. Key control
   1. Great grand master   S_____   U_____   NA_____
   2. Grand master   S_____   U_____   NA_____
   3. Master   S_____   U_____   NA_____
   4. Individual   S_____   U_____   NA_____
   5. Zone control   S_____   U_____   NA_____
   6. Assignment list   S_____   U_____   NA_____
   7. Restrictions   S_____   U_____   NA_____
   8. Other _____   S_____   U_____   NA_____
   9. Comments _____
G. Security Systems
   1. Electronic   S_____   U_____   NA_____
   2. Trailer   S_____   U_____   NA_____
   3. Fences   S_____   U_____   NA_____
   4. Locking systems   S_____   U_____   NA_____
   5. Other _____   S_____   U_____   NA_____
   6. Comments _____
        _____

H. Classrooms
1. Windows   S_____ U_____ NA_____
2. Interior doors   S_____ U_____ NA_____
3. Exterior doors   S_____ U_____ NA_____
4. Windows in doors   S_____ U_____ NA_____
5. Proprietary space   S_____ U_____ NA_____
6. Multiple purpose   S_____ U_____ NA_____
7. Other _____ S_____ U_____ NA_____
8. Comments _____

_____

I. High-value areas (doors, windows, locks, location procedures)
1. Computers   S_____ U_____ NA_____
2. Business machines   S_____ U_____ NA_____
3. Audio/visual   S_____ U_____ NA_____
4. Shop/vocational   S_____ U_____ NA_____
5. Other _____ S_____ U_____ NA_____
6. Comments _____

_____

J. Corridors
1. Lockers   S_____ U_____ NA_____
2. Lighting   S_____ U_____ NA_____
3. Surveillance
    General   S_____ U_____ NA_____
    Classrooms   S_____ U_____ NA_____
    Officers   S_____ U_____ NA_____
4. Shop/vocational   S_____ U_____ NA_____
5. Other_____ S_____ U_____ NA_____
6. Comments _____

_____

K. Stairwells
1. Interior   S_____ U_____ NA_____
2. Exterior   S_____ U_____ NA_____
3. Fire   S_____ U_____ NA_____
4. Comments _____

_____

L. Restrooms
1. Location(s)   S_____ U_____ NA_____
2. Entrance design   S_____ U_____ NA_____
3. Interior access   S_____ U_____ NA_____
4. Other _____ S_____ U_____ NA_____
5. Comments _____

_____

M. Locker room(s)
    1. Location(s)   S_____ U_____ NA_____
    2. Surveillance
         Interior   S_____ U_____ NA_____
         Exterior   S_____ U_____ NA_____
    3. Doors   S_____ U_____ NA_____
    4. Windows   S_____ U_____ NA_____
    5. Equipment storage   S_____ U_____ NA_____
    6. Lockers
         Layout   S_____ U_____ NA_____
         Assignment   S_____ U_____ NA_____
    7. Other _____   S_____ U_____ NA_____
    8. Comments _____
_____

N. Cafeteria
    1. Equipment   S_____ U_____ NA_____
    2. Storage   S_____ U_____ NA_____
    3. Queuing   S_____ U_____ NA_____
    4. Table arrangements   S_____ U_____ NA_____
    5. Surveillance   S_____ U_____ NA_____
    6. Patio/gathering area access S_____ U_____ NA_____
    7. Other _____   S_____ U_____ NA_____
    8. Comments _____
_____

O. Other areas
    1. Portables   S_____ U_____ NA_____
    2. Athletic/recreational   S_____ U_____ NA_____
    3. Storage   S_____ U_____ NA_____
    4. _____   S_____ U_____ NA_____
    5. _____   S_____ U_____ NA_____
    6. _____   S_____ U_____ NA_____
    7. Comments _____
_____

P. Administrative
    1. Inventory control   S_____ U_____ NA_____
    2. Facility management   S_____ U_____ NA_____
         Scheduling   S_____ U_____ NA_____
         Hours   S_____ U_____ NA_____
         Functional layout   S_____ U_____ NA_____
         Productivity   S_____ U_____ NA_____
         Surveillance   S_____ U_____ NA_____
    3. Maintenance   S_____ U_____ NA_____
    4. Programs   S_____ U_____ NA_____
         Incentive   S_____ U_____ NA_____

Student patrol   S_____   U_____   NA_____

      Other _____   S_____   U_____   NA_____

5. Staff   S_____   U_____   NA_____

      Hall duty   S_____   U_____   NA_____

      Planning areas   S_____   U_____   NA_____

      Other _____   S_____   U_____   NA_____

6. Comments _____

_____

V. Priority Recommendations

A. Physical space

1. Remove _____

_____

2. Repair _____

_____

3. Replace _____

_____

4. Install _____

_____

5. Reallocate _____

_____

6. Other _____

_____

B. Management (policy, procedure, personnel allocation, neighborhood programs, or other)

_____

_____

VI. Security Plan

A. Neighborhood _____

_____

B. Perimeter _____

_____

C. Grounds _____

_____

D. Parking (vehicle and bicycle) _____

_____

E. Building access _____
_____

F. Building exterior _____
_____

G. Building interior (classrooms, corridors, restrooms, offices) _____
_____

H. High-value areas _____
_____

I. Protection of persons _____
_____

J. Special events _____
_____

K. Other _____
_____

VII. School Incident Map: Target Incidents

		Last year	Year-to-date
1.	Breaking and entering	_____	_____
2.	Vandalism	_____	_____
3.	Theft	_____	_____
4.	Arson/fire	_____	_____
5.	Staff assault	_____	_____
6.	Assault/battery	_____	_____
7.	Sex offense	_____	_____
8.	Drugs/alcohol	_____	_____
9.	Bomb	_____	_____
10.	Weapons	_____	_____

Adapted from School Security Survey Form, TDC & Associates.
Developed by Tim Crowe, TDC & Associates, 14508 Ashmont Place, Louisville, KY 40223.

Student School Safety Survey I

Directions: We would like to have your opinion on issues related to school safety. Your answers will help us in our discussions about improving the school. **Please do not write your name on this survey.**

Demographics:

1. Sex: _____ Male   _____ Female

2. Race/ethnicity: _____ White, non-Hispanic   _____ African-American, non-Hispanic
   _____ Hispanic   _____ Native American or Alaskan Native
   _____ Asian or Pacific Islander   _____ Other _____

3. Grade in school: _____ 9th   _____ 10th
   _____ 11th   _____ 12th

4. In your opinion, what are the three major issues concerning physical safety at your school right now?

   1. _____

   2. _____

   3. _____

Please read the following statements. Mark the answer that best describes your feelings about each statement, circling whether you strongly agree (SA), agree (A), disagree (D), strongly disagree (SD), or don't know (DK).

5. Students of all racial groups at school get along with each other.   SA   A   D   SD   DK

6. Students of all racial groups at my school work out their problems with each other.   SA   A   D   SD   DK

7. The views and opinions of students are respected and listened to by teachers at my school. SA   A   D   SD   DK

8. The views and opinions of students are respected and listened to by administrators at my school. SA   A   D   SD   DK

9. School rules are clearly defined and explained so that I understand them.   SA   A   D   SD   DK

10. School rules are fairly and consistently enforced for all students.   SA   A   D   SD   DK

11. Gangs cause trouble at my school.   SA   A   D   SD   DK

12. I feel comfortable telling teachers or administrators about potential fights or arguments at school. SA   A   D   SD   DK

13. I feel comfortable telling teachers or administrators about drugs at school.	SA	A	D	SD	DK
14. I feel it is my responsibility to tell teachers or administrators about drugs at school when I learn about it.	SA	A	D	SD	DK
15. I feel comfortable telling teachers or administrators about weapons at school.	SA	A	D	SD	DK
16. Teachers show respect to students.	SA	A	D	SD	DK
17. Teachers show that they care about students.	SA	A	D	SD	DK
18. Students show respect to teachers.	SA	A	D	SD	DK

19. Are there particular places at school where you feel unsafe? ____Yes _____ No

If yes, write them below and check the times of the day when these places seem unsafe.

Place on Campus	Before School	During Class	During Lunch	After School	All Day	Other
_____	_____	_____	_____	_____	_____	_____
_____	_____	_____	_____	_____	_____	_____
_____	_____	_____	_____	_____	_____	_____

Please complete the following to reflect your experience at your school or on the school bus this school year.

20. I have had things stolen from my:				
_____ Desk	Never	1-2 times	3-4 times	5+ times
_____ Locker	Never	1-2 times	3-4 times	5+ times
_____ Other_____	Never	1-2 times	3-4 Times	5+ times
21. I have had money or things taken from me by force.	Never	1-2 times	3-4 times	5+ times
22. I have had money or things taken from me by use of a weapon.	Never	1-2 times	3-4 times	5+ times
23. I have been physically threatened.	Never	1-2 times	3-4 times	5+ times
24. I have been physically attacked.	Never	1-2 times	3-4 times	5+ times
25. I have been physically injured.	Never	1-2 times	3-4 times	5+ times
26. I have had unwelcome sexual advances made to me.	Never	1-2 times	3-4 times	5+ times
27. I have had attempts at sexual assault on me.	Never	1-2 times	3-4 times	5+ times
28. I have been sexually assaulted.	Never	1-2 times	3-4 times	5+ times
29. I have witnessed fights at school.	Never	1-2 times	3-4 times	5+ times
30. I have witnessed fights on the school bus.	Never	1-2 times	3-4 times	5+ times
31. I have seen students carrying a weapon at school.	Never	1-2 times	3-4 times	5+ times
32. I have seen students carrying a weapon on the school bus.	Never	1-2 times	3-4 times	5+ times

Thank you for answering these questions.

Safe Schools: A Handbook for Violence Prevention

Student School Safety Survey II

This survey asks about your views on safety and crime on your campus. **Do not write your name on this survey. The answers you give will be kept private.** Circle only one answer for each question, unless you are given other instructions. (This survey may be given verbally to younger students.)

1. Sex: _____ Male _____ Female

2. Race/ethnicity:
   _____ White, non-Hispanic _____ African-American, non-Hispanic
   _____ Hispanic _____ Native American or Alaskan Native
   _____ Asian or Pacific Islander _____ Other _____

3. Grade in school:
   | Pre-K | 1 | 2 | 3 | 4 | 5 | 6 |
   | K | 7 | 8 | 9 | 10 | 11 | 12 |

4. How safe do you feel at school?
   very safe   safe   unsafe

5a. Are there particular places at school where you don't feel safe? If there are, where are they?
   _____
   _____

5b. Are there certain times of day when these places are unsafe?
   before school   during class   during lunch
   after school   entire school day
   other:_____

6. This school year, have you had something stolen from your desk, locker, or other place at school?
   never   one to two times   three to four times   more than four times

7. This school year, has someone taken money or things directly from you by using force, weapons, or threats at school?
   never   one to two times   three to four times   more than four times

8. This school year, has someone physically threatened, attacked, or hurt you at school?
   never   one to two times   three to four times   more than four times

9a. This school year, has someone verbally threatened you at school?
   never   one to two times   three to four times   more than four times

9b. If yes, please specify where this happened to you.
   at school   to and from school   on a school bus   at a school-sponsored activity
   other_____

10a. This school year, has someone made sexual advances or attempted to sexually assault you at school?
   never   one to two times   three to four times   more than four times

10b. This school year, has someone sexually assaulted you at school?
   never   one to two times   three to four times   more than four times

11a. Is there a process in place for students to report alleged physical, psychological, or sexual abuse?

        yes   no

11b. Does the campus follow up on reports of alleged abuse?

        yes   no

12a. Have you ever seen a student carrying a weapon at school?

        yes   no

12b. If yes, please specify what kind of weapon you saw:

_____

_____

13. During this school year, how many fights have you witnessed at your school?

        none   one to two   three to four   more than four

14. In your opinion, how serious are the following problems at school?

	Don't Know	No Problem	Small Problem	Serious Problem
a. Vandalism, including graffiti	0	1	2	3
b. Gangs	0	1	2	3
c. Alcohol use	0	1	2	3
d. Tobacco use	0	1	2	3
e. Drug use	0	1	2	3
f. Drug selling	0	1	2	3
g. Carrying weapons	0	1	2	3
h. Racial conflict	0	1	2	3
i. Other _____				

15. In your opinion, what are the three major safety or crime problems at school right now?

    a. _____

    b. _____

    c. _____

Thank you for answering these questions.

Parent School Safety Survey

Your campus is currently reviewing its safety programs and policies. The administration is interested in your views and the problems you feel need to be addressed. Please circle only one answer unless otherwise instructed. **Do not put your name on this survey. Responses will be reported to the school in summary form only.**

1. Sex: _____ Male _____ Female

2. Race/ethnicity: _____ White, non-Hispanic _____ African-American, non-Hispanic
    _____ Hispanic _____ Native American or Alaskan Native
    _____ Asian or Pacific Islander _____ Other _____

3. Number of your children who are enrolled on this campus: _____

4. Grade(s) of your children at this campus: (Circle all that apply.)
    Pre-K   1   2   3   4   5   6
    K   7   8   9   10   11   12

5. How safe does your child feel at school?
    very safe   safe   unsafe

6a. Are there particular places at school where your child/children don't feel safe? If there are, where are they?
    _____
    _____

6b. Are there certain times of day when these places are unsafe?
    before school   during class   during lunch   after school   entire school day
    other:_____

7. This school year, has your child had something stolen from his/her desk, locker, or other place at school?
    never   one to two times   three to four times   more than four times

8. This school year, has someone taken money or things directly from your child by using force, weapons, or threats at school?
    never   one to two times   three to four times   more than four times

9. This school year, has someone physically threatened, attacked, or hurt your child at school?
    never   one to two times   three to four times   more than four times

10a. This school year, has someone verbally threatened your child at school?
    never   one to two times   three to four times   more than four times

10b. If yes, please specify where this happened to your child.
    at school   to and from school   on a school bus   at a school-sponsored activity
    other_____

11a. This school year, has someone made sexual advances or attempted to sexually assault your child at school?
    never   one to two times   three to four times   more than four times

11b. This school year, has someone sexually assaulted your child at school?
    never   one to two times   three to four times   more than four times

12a. Is there a process in place for students to report alleged physical, psychological, or sexual abuse?
      yes   no

12b. Does the campus follow up on reports of alleged abuse?
      yes   no

13a. During this school year, has your child talked about seeing a student carrying a weapon at school?
      yes   no

13b. If yes, please specify what kind of weapon your child saw:
_____
_____

14. During this school year, how many fights has your child witnessed at your school?
      none   one or two   three to four   more than four

15. In your opinion, how serious are the following problems at school?

	Don't Know	No Problem	Small Problem	Serious Problem
a. Vandalism, including graffiti	0	1	2	3
b. Gangs	0	1	2	3
c. Alcohol use	0	1	2	3
d. Tobacco use	0	1	2	3
e. Drug use	0	1	2	3
f. Drug selling	0	1	2	3
g. Carrying weapons	0	1	2	3
h. Racial conflict	0	1	2	3
i. Other_____				

16. In your opinion, what are the three major safety or crime problems at school right now?
    a. _____
    b. _____
    c. _____

Thank you for answering these questions.

Teacher School Safety Survey

This survey asks about your views on safety and crime on your campus. **Do not write your name on this survey. The answers you give will be kept private. Items 1, 2, and 3 are optional.** Circle only one answer for each question, unless you are given other instructions.

1. Sex: _____ Male   _____ Female

2. Race/Ethnicity: _____ White, non-Hispanic   _____ African-American, non-Hispanic
                     _____ Hispanic   _____ Native American or Alaskan Native
                     _____ Asian or Pacific Islander   _____ Other _____

3. What is the grade level or level of courses that you teach? (Circle all that apply.)

Pre-K	1	2	3	4	5	6
K	7	8	9	10	11	12

4. How safe do you feel at school?
    very safe   safe   unsafe

5a. Are there particular places at school where you don't feel safe? If there are, where are they?
    _____
    _____

5b. Are there certain times of day when these places are unsafe?
    before school   during class   during lunch   after school   entire school day
    other:_____

6. This school year, have you had something stolen from your desk, locker, or other place at school?
    never   one to two times   three to four times   more than four times

7. This school year, has someone taken money or things directly from you by using force, weapons or threats at school?
    never   one to two times   three to four times   more than four times

8. This school year, has your personal property been damaged while on school property or at school-sponsored events?
    never   one to two times   three to four times   more than four times

9. This school year, has someone physically threatened, attacked, or hurt you at school?
    never   one to two times   three to four times   more than four times

10. This school year, have you been verbally abused at school?
    never   one to two times   three to four times   more than four times

11a. This school year, has someone made sexual advances or attempted to sexually assault you at school?
    never   one to two times   three to four times   more than four times

11b. This school year, has someone sexually assaulted you at school?
    never   one to two times   three to four times   more than four times

12a. Is there a process in place for students to report alleged physical, psychological, or sexual abuse?
        yes   no

12b. Does the campus follow up on reports of alleged abuse?
        yes   no

13. Do gangs cause trouble at your school?
        yes   sometimes   no   don't know   no gangs at my school

14a. Have you ever seen a student carrying a weapon at school?
        yes   no

14b. If yes, please specify what kind of weapon you saw:

_____

_____

15. During this school year, how many fights have you witnessed at your school?
        none   one to two   three to four   more than four

16. In your opinion, how serious are the following problems at school?

	Don't Know	No Problem	Small Problem	Serious Problem
a. Vandalism, including graffiti	0	1	2	3
b. Gangs	0	1	2	3
c. Alcohol use	0	1	2	3
d. Tobacco use	0	1	2	3
e. Drug use	0	1	2	3
f. Drug selling	0	1	2	3
g. Carrying weapons	0	1	2	3
h. Racial conflict	0	1	2	3
i. Other _____				

17. In your opinion, what are the three major safety or crime problems at school right now?
    a. _____
    b. _____
    c. _____

Thank you for answering these questions.

Teacher Discipline and Classroom Management
Self-Assessment

The Teacher Discipline and Classroom Management Self-Assessment is based on the Assertive Discipline Direct Teaching Model for classroom management. This model essentially focuses on the establishment and maintenance of the teacher's authority and effectiveness in controlling student behavior. If your school is following this model, then this instrument can be used to identify teacher strengths and weaknesses that are consistent with this model.

Purpose: This assessment is designed to help you, as a teacher, identify strengths and weaknesses in your classroom management and discipline style.

Directions: Read the statements and put a check on the line that best represents how frequently you display this classroom behavior. (U = Usually; S = Sometimes; N = Never)

	U	S	N
1. I give clear and specific instructions.	—	—	—
2. I use a variety of cues to remind students of expected behavior.	—	—	—
3. I teach students my cues.	—	—	—
4. I communicate positive expectations of good behavior to my class.	—	—	—
5. I have clear and specific rules that I teach my students.	—	—	—
6. I respond to behaviors I like with specific, personal praise.	—	—	—
7. I consistently follow through with consequences to enforce rules.	—	—	—

My students have trouble:

	U	S	N
8. following my instructions.	—	—	—
9. understanding my instructions.	—	—	—
10. accepting instructions from me.	—	—	—
11. solving conflicts with other students.	—	—	—
12. solving conflicts with me.	—	—	—
13. staying focused on a topic.	—	—	—
14. listening during class.	—	—	—
15. other _____	—	—	—

I have trouble:

	U	S	N
16. giving directions.	—	—	—
17. instructing large groups.	—	—	—
18. instructing small groups.	—	—	—
19. instructing individual students.	—	—	—
20. teaching new concepts.	—	—	—

My discipline problems occur:

	U	S	N
21. within my classroom.	—	—	—
22. when I am responsible for students outside my classroom.	—	—	—

	U	S	N
23. when students are making the transition to my classroom.	—	—	—
24. I spend too much time on discipline.	—	—	—

I am afraid or uncomfortable around students because of their:

	U	S	N
25 race	—	—	—
26. size	—	—	—
27. cultural background	—	—	—
28. socio-economic background	—	—	—
29. sex	—	—	—

	U	S	N
30. I feel comfortable disciplining all of my students.	—	—	—

Which of these three approaches to discipline are you comfortable with?

	U	S	N
31. direct intervention/authority	—	—	—
32. teacher-student interaction/discussion	—	—	—
33. providing opportunities for students to shape disciplinary actions	—	—	—

Which of these three approaches do you use in disciplining students?

	U	S	N
34. direct intervention/authority	—	—	—
35. teacher-student interaction/discussion	—	—	—
36. providing opportunities for students to shape disciplinary actions	—	—	—

	U	S	N
37. I can identify discipline problems in functional (behavioral/observable) terms.	—	—	—
38. I can identify probable causes for discipline problems.	—	—	—
39. My interventions are consistent with the causes of discipline problems.	—	—	—
40. I have a good understanding of the classroom management options available to me.	—	—	—
41. My classroom management style allows me to meet the educational needs of all students.	—	—	—
42. My classroom management style allows me to address the discipline problems of individual students.	—	—	—

Questions 1–7 from Discipline Self-Test for Classroom Teachers, *Phi Delta Kappan*, Vol. 68 (No. 1), p. 66, 1986.

Quality Management in the Classroom Checklist:
Teacher Self-Assessment

The Quality Management in the Classroom Checklist is based on a quality management model for classroom management. This teacher quality model essentially proposes that each student is endowed with unique gifts and contributions, has the capability and desire to learn, and that teachers work with students to create an environment that makes learning meaningful and enjoyable. If your school is moving towards implementing a quality management model, then this instrument is useful for assessing teachers' progress in creating a quality environment for student learning.

Purpose: This checklist is based on a quality management model for classroom management. The purpose of this checklist is to identify a series of items that you can use to assess your classroom management style in terms of the quality management model.

Directions: Read the statements below. Please respond to each statement twice, once for how things are now and the second time for how you would like things to be. Check the line for **A** if you agree with the statement and **D** if you disagree.

STATEMENT	How Things Are Now		How Things Should Be	
	A	D	A	D
1. I treat students with respect.	___	___	___	___
2. Parents are welcome in my class.	___	___	___	___
3. I respect teachers from other subject areas.	___	___	___	___
4. I like my students.	___	___	___	___
5. While my students don't always agree, we share concerns with each other openly.	___	___	___	___
6. I feel I am a good spokesperson for my class.	___	___	___	___
7. I make students enthusiastic about learning.	___	___	___	___
8. I am enthusiastic about learning.	___	___	___	___
9. I feel pride in this school and its students.	___	___	___	___
10. I develop and maintain a high level of morale.	___	___	___	___
11. Important decisions are made in this classroom by a team process.	___	___	___	___
12. I am seeking new ideas.	___	___	___	___
13. There is a "we" spirit in this classroom.	___	___	___	___
14. My students and I collaborate toward making the classroom run effectively with little teacher-student tension.	___	___	___	___
15. I consider differences between individuals and groups (both teacher and students) to contribute to the richness of the class.	___	___	___	___
16. When a problem comes up, the class has procedures for working on it.	___	___	___	___

STATEMENT	How Things Are Now		How Things Should Be	
	A	D	A	D
17. I see problems as normal challenges and not as "rocking the boat."	—	—	—	—
18. I encourage students to be creative rather than to conform in the classroom.	—	—	—	—
19. I really care about students.	—	—	—	—
20. I try to deal with conflict constructively not just "keep the lid on."	—	—	—	—
21. When there are classroom conflicts, the result is constructive and never destructive.	—	—	—	—
22. In my class there is communication between groups.	—	—	—	—
23. Problems in my class are recognized and worked upon openly. They are not allowed to slide.	—	—	—	—
24. People in my class solve problems, they don't just talk about them.	—	—	—	—
25. In my class, students with ideas or values different from the commonly accepted ones get a chance to be heard.	—	—	—	—
26. I believe there may be several alternative solutions to most problems.	—	—	—	—
27. Students from my class take responsibility for their own learning.	—	—	—	—
28. Students from my class know how to resolve their own problems.	—	—	—	—
29. My class fosters a sense of teamwork, and everyone wants to help others.	—	—	—	—
30. Students feel pride in my class.	—	—	—	—
31. I share information and ideas with colleagues.	—	—	—	—
32. I display a sense of teamwork among colleagues, students and parents for purposes of student success.	—	—	—	—

Adapted with permission from *Implementing Total Quality Management in the Classroom*, by Byrnes, Cornesky and Byrnes, 1992, Cornesky & Associates Press, pp. 89-90.

Interview Questions for Security Officers

District _____   Officer Name(s) _____ (Optional)
School _____   Date _____

1. How long have you been a security officer at this school?

2. Please tell me about the role that you play in the School Security Enhancement Program.
   Probes: What services are provided?
              How are the services provided?
              When are services provided (e.g., all day, after school)?
              What are your duties as a security officer?
              Are there special techniques that you use to carry out the duties?
              What techniques have worked particularly well?

3. Do you or the other security staff provide supervision in the following areas?

	Yes	No
a. School bus loading/unloading area	1	2
b. Hallways	1	2
c. School grounds	1	2
d. Cafeterias	1	2
e. Parking lots	1	2
f. After-school functions (e.g., dances and sports)	1	2
g. Other (specify): _____		

4. During the current school year at this school, how often does the security staff investigate incidents relating to:

	Less than once/month	More than once/month	About once/week	More than once/week
a. Vandalism	1	2	3	4
b. Theft	1	2	3	4
c. Student possessing/using weapons	1	2	3	4
d. Student drug possession	1	2	3	4
e. Drug sales	1	2	3	4
f. Gang activity	1	2	3	4
g. Assault	1	2	3	4
h. Student referral to school administration	1	2	3	4
i. Student referral to other agencies	1	2	3	4
j. Other (specify): _____	1	2	3	4

5. How closely does the security staff work with personnel in other programs or agencies?

	No Involvement	Communication Only	Some Cooperation	Working Closely
a. Intervention specialist	1	2	3	4
b. Local police	1	2	3	4
c. Child Protective Services staff	1	2	3	4
d. Juvenile justice	1	2	3	4
e. Community-based organizations	1	2	3	4
f. Other (specify): _____	1	2	3	4

6. Are you and the other security staff at this school hired by the school district or an outside agency?

7. To what degree is the school security program integrated with the student assistance program? How does service integration occur?
Probe: How do you work with the intervention specialist?

8. In your view, are the security staff receiving support and cooperation from school administrators and school staff?

9. What makes your job (as a security officer) difficult at this school?

10. What can be done to address or resolve these difficulties?

11. What suggestions do you have for improving the school security program?

12. Compared with last year, do you think this school is safer this year?
Probe: Why do you think so?

13. Do you have other comments or observations about the program or school safety in general?

This survey is from the Washington State Omnibus Alcohol and Controlled Substance Act: Enhancement of School-Based Security Program, A Statewide Evaluation of Washington's School Security Enhancement Program.

Security Maintenance Checklist

Purpose: This Security Maintenance Checklist is an extensive series of items developed by the Florida Department of Law Enforcement (FDLE). There are a total of nine survey sections covering the security of windows, doors, miscellaneous openings and outbuildings, key control, lighting and electrical boxes, perimeter and grounds, access control procedures, property identification and inventory control, and alarms.

These nine subsections are concluded by a final page containing statements on the frequency with which security maintenance items are checked. This page can also be used to set a schedule for conducting security maintenance checks if you decide they are needed.

Directions: Place a check on the line that best represents the current status of security maintenance at your school. Use this information as input into your school discussions on prioritizing needs for school improvement.

SECTION I — Windows

Criteria for Security: All ground floor windows must meet the following criteria. Depending on their accessibility to an intruder, some windows above the ground floor must also meet the criteria.
   a. Locking hardware is in proper working order.
   b. Opening is protected with burglar-resistant glazing or decorative grill; broken windows are normally replaced with burglar-resistant glazing.
   c. Additional security is provided for window openings with air conditioning units.
   d. Base windows are protected with security grill or well cover.

(Note: The Life Safety Code requires that each room have at least one window which can be used for emergency rescue.)

Directions: Read the statements below and check the appropriate line. If you check "No," please explain why in the space provided.

	Yes	No	If No, Explain
All ground-floor and other accessible windows are secure.	___	___	_____

SECTION II — Doors

Criteria for Security: All exterior doors must meet the following criteria. Where security is required on interior doors, they must also meet the same criteria. An example of an interior door where security is needed would be the AV storage room in the media center.
   a. Locking hardware is in proper working order.
   b. Framework is strong, and door fits snugly.
   c. Strike plate is strong and securely affixed.
   d. No breakable glass (in door or sidelights) within 40 inches of panic bar or button.
   e. Door cannot be bypassed, e.g., through transom or decorative paneling above door.

f. Panic bar (or button) operates properly.

g. Exposed hinge pins on outswing doors cannot be easily removed.

h. The inactive (stationary) left on double doors is secured at both top and bottom.

i. Overhead door is secured with auxiliary locking device.

j. Portals and hatches are secured with heavy-duty hasp and padlock.

k. Key numbers have been removed from all padlocks.

l. Exterior doors equipped with panic bars are secured with heavy-duty chain and padlock at night and on weekends.

m. Outside handles are removed from doors used only as exits.

(NOTE: Safety requirements never allow the use of chain and padlock when building is occupied.)

Directions: Read the statements and check the appropriate line. If you check "No" please explain why in the space provided.

	Yes	No	If No, Explain
Outside entrances are secure.	___	___	_____
Inside doors are secure.	___	___	_____
Overhead doors are secure.	___	___	_____
Portals and hatches are secure.	___	___	_____

SECTION III — Miscellaneous Openings and Outbuildings

Criteria for Security: All openings and exterior barriers must be checked for adequate security. Particular attention must be given to roof hatches, cornices above protective porches, and sheds containing combustible or expensive maintenance or athletic equipment.

Directions: Read the statements and check the appropriate box. If you check "No," please explain why in the space provided.

	Yes	No	If No, Explain
Openings accessible to intruders are secure.	___	___	_____
Outbuildings, storage sheds, and portable classrooms are secure.	___	___	_____
Walls and fixtures in unsupervised hangout areas are durable and well protected.	___	___	_____
Portals and hatches are secure.	___	___	_____

SECTION IV —Key Control

Criteria for Security: Optimum security is contingent upon a proper control system for keys. Minimum criteria to be met are:

    a. The responsibility for lock and key control is assigned to a single individual.

    b. All file keys and duplicates are kept in a steel key cabinet, under lock and key.

    c. All keys are maintained and issued with strict supervision, including the requirement that each key issued must be signed for (using key receipt tags).

    d. Master keys are kept to a minimum and are retained by top administrative personnel only (principal, assistant principal, and maintenance supervisor).

    e. Appropriate fines or penalties are enforced when an employee loses a key.

    f. Employees are never permitted to have a duplicate key made on their own.

    g. Keys are always collected from employees who terminate or transfer.

    h. All keys are collected and logged at the conclusion of the school year; the key control system is re-evaluated and inadequacies are corrected before keys are reissued.

    i. Tumblers in vital locks are changed if keys are permanently lost or stolen.

Directions: Read the statements and check the appropriate line. If you check "No," please explain why in the space provided.

	Yes	No	If No, Explain
The key control system is adequate.	___	___	_____
The key cabinet is maintained with sufficient number of hooks, tags, and supervision.	___	___	_____

SECTION V — Lighting and Electrical Boxes

Directions: Appropriate use of lighting can greatly increase the security of a school campus. Read the statements and check the appropriate line. If you check "No," please explain why in the space provided.

	Yes	No	If No, Explain
The perimeter of the school building is protected by adequate lighting.	___	___	_____
Repairs to lights and replacement of inoperative lamps are made immediately.	___	___	_____
There is sufficient light to provide marginal coverage in case a bulb burns out.	___	___	_____
Photoelectric cells are located out of reach of spotlights.	___	___	_____

	Yes	No	If No, Explain
All accessible lenses are protected by some unbreakable material.	__	__	_____
Additional lighting is provided at entrances and other points of possible intrusion.	__	__	_____
The wiring for protective lighting is properly mounted.	__	__	_____
Switches and controls are properly located and protected.	__	__	_____
The lighting system is designed and location of fixtures is recorded so that repairs could be made rapidly.	__	__	_____
Materials and equipment in storage areas are properly arranged to provide adequate lighting.	__	__	_____
The possibility of lower energy consumption and higher lighting levels with more efficient light sources has been explored.	__	__	_____
Corridors and stairwells are properly lighted for safety.	__	__	_____
Directional lights are aimed at the building rather than away from it.	__	__	_____
Access to electrical panels is restricted.	__	__	_____
Mechanical rooms and other hazardous storage areas are kept locked.	__	__	_____

SECTION VI — Perimeter and Grounds

Directions: Read the statements and check the appropriate line. If you check "No," please explain why in the space provided.

Fencing:	Yes	No	If No, Explain
The school grounds are fenced.	__	__	_____
The fencing is high enough so that intruders cannot easily jump over it.	__	__	_____
Trees and telephone poles are far enough away from the fence so that they cannot be used for entrance or exit.	__	__	_____

Safe Schools: A Handbook for Violence Prevention

	Yes	No	If No, Explain
The gates are well constructed.	—	—	_____
Gates are secured by functioning padlocks or chains.	—	—	_____

Visibility and Access:

	Yes	No	If No, Explain
All areas of the school buildings and grounds are accessible to cruising police vehicles.	—	—	_____
Buildings are visible to passing patrol cars.	—	—	_____
Access to bus loading areas has been restricted for other vehicles.	—	—	_____
School personnel have been assigned to bus loading/drop-off areas.	—	—	_____
School personnel have been assigned to student parking areas during arrival and dismissal times.	—	—	_____

Vandalism and Theft Prevention:

School grounds should meet the following criteria:

    a. Grounds are mowed and free from debris.
    b. Exterior and interior walls are free from graffiti.
    c. Floors are kept clean, and damaged floor covering is replaced promptly.
    d. Broken glass is replaced promptly with Plexiglas or other break-resistant material.

	Yes	No	If No, Explain
School facilities are generally kept neat and in good repair.	—	—	_____
Sections of the building are locked when not in use for specific after-hours activities.	—	—	_____
Protective screens or window guards have been installed in areas where glass is frequently broken.	—	—	_____
School files and records are maintained in locked, vandal-proof, fireproof containers or vaults.	—	—	_____
The school maintains a record of all maintenance on doors, windows, lockers, and other areas of the school.	—	—	_____

	Yes	No	If No, Explain
Graffiti is photographed (to record possible gang identification) and removed promptly.	___	___	_____
All items that could be used to break into the building have been removed from school grounds.	___	___	_____
Driver education vehicles are secure.	___	___	_____

Playground Safety:	Yes	No	If No, Explain
Vehicle access to play areas is restricted.	___	___	_____
All play areas are fenced.	___	___	_____
Bicycle racks are provided in a location which allows for good visual surveillance.	___	___	_____
Playground equipment is located so as to permit good visual surveillance by school staff.	___	___	_____
Playground equipment has tamper-proof fasteners.	___	___	_____

SECTION VII — Access Control Procedures

Directions: Read the statements and check the appropriate box. If you check "No," please explain why in the space provided.

Visitors:	Yes	No	If No, Explain
There are written regulations regarding the access and control of visitors to the school.	___	___	_____
Signs concerning visitor policy and trespassing are properly displayed at all entrances to the campus and buildings.	___	___	_____
Clearly marked visitor parking is provided as close to the main office as possible and/or in a high-visibility location.	___	___	_____
School personnel are assigned to duty stations on the school grounds when school is in session.	___	___	_____

	Yes	No	If No, Explain
Personnel assigned to duty stations have two-way communication with the main office.	—	—	_____
All visitors are greeted upon entering the school.	—	—	_____
One entrance is designated for visitors.	—	—	_____
There are signs on other entrances requesting visitors to use only the designated entrance.	—	—	_____
The school office area is located near the main entrance.	—	—	_____
Visitors are required to sign in.	—	—	_____
Visitors are issued identification cards or badges.	—	—	_____
Deliveries are made at one entrance designated for this purpose.	—	—	_____
Delivery persons are always accompanied by a staff person when carrying supplies into the kitchen, storeroom, or other areas.	—	—	_____
There is a policy for intercepting/responding to suspicious persons observed on school grounds.	—	—	_____

Students:	Yes	No	If No, Explain
There are written regulations restricting student access to school grounds and buildings.	—	—	_____
Students are issued ID cards or other identification.	—	—	_____
Students are issued parking stickers for assigned parking areas.	—	—	_____
Student access to parking areas is restricted to arrival and dismissal times.	—	—	_____
A parking area has been designated for students who must leave school during the day.	—	—	_____
"Restricted" areas are properly identified.	—	—	_____

	Yes	No	If No, Explain
Students are required to carry a pass when exempted from attendance of classes.	___	___	_____
Students are restricted from loitering in corridors, hallways, and restrooms.	___	___	_____
Students are restricted from entering vacant classrooms alone.	___	___	_____
Friends, relatives, or non-custodial parents are required to have written permission to pick up a student from school.	___	___	_____
Students are required to have written permission to leave school during school hours.	___	___	_____
A high visibility area has been designated as the pickup/drop-off point for students.	___	___	_____
Student parking areas are located to permit easy surveillance by school staff.	___	___	_____
Student lockers are located in areas which allow for easy surveillance by school staff.	___	___	_____

Staff:	Yes	No	If No, Explain
Full- and part-time staff, including bus drivers, are issued ID cards or other identification.	___	___	_____
There are written regulations regarding access and control of school personnel after school hours.	___	___	_____
Staff members who remain after school hours are required to sign out.	___	___	_____
Faculty members are required to lock classrooms upon leaving.	___	___	_____
One person is designated to perform the following security checks at the end of the day:			
• Check that all classrooms and offices are locked.	___	___	_____

	Yes	No	If No, Explain

- Check all restrooms and locker rooms to ensure that no one is hiding.   ___ ___ _____
- Check all exterior entrances to ensure that they are locked.   ___ ___ _____
- Check all night lights to ensure that they have been turned on.   ___ ___ _____
- Check the alarm system to ensure that it is functioning properly.   ___ ___ _____

The telephone number of the principal is provided to the police department so that police can make contact in an emergency situation.   ___ ___ _____

There is two-way communication between the office and all classrooms, including portable units.   ___ ___ _____

A school resource officer is assigned to the school.   ___ ___ _____

Law enforcement personnel or community residents monitor school grounds after school hours.   ___ ___ _____

SECTION VIII —Property Identification and Inventory Control

Directions: Read the statements and check the appropriate line. If you check "No," please explain why in the space provided.

	Yes	No	If No, Explain

All school equipment has been permanently marked with Operation Identification Numbers.   ___ ___ _____

Operation ID warning stickers have been placed at all entrances and on marked items.   ___ ___ _____

An up-to-date inventory of all school equipment is maintained.   ___ ___ _____

A perpetual inventory is maintained for all expendable school supplies.   ___ ___ _____

Secure storage is available during and after school for valuable items.   ___ ___ _____

Special security measures have been taken for high-target items.   ___ ___ _____

	Yes	No	If No, Explain
Cash is deposited in the bank daily.	__	__	_____

SECTION IX — Alarms

Directions: Read the statements and check the appropriate line. If you check "No," please explain why in the space provided.

If the school has no alarm system:	Yes	No	If No, Explain
Is an alarm system necessary?	__	__	_____

(describe system recommended)_____

_____

Recommended Type(s) _____
Recommended Location(s)_____

	Yes	No	If No, Explain
Sensors (Detectors)	__	__	_____
Contact Switches			
Photoelectric	__	__	_____
Passive Infrared	__	__	_____
Sound Monitoring	__	__	_____
Digital Dialer	__	__	_____
Voice Dialer	__	__	_____
Signal Transmission	__	__	_____
Leased Lines	__	__	_____
Comments and Recommendations:	__	__	_____

_____

If the school is protected by an alarm system:	Yes	No	If No, Explain
There is regular maintenance and/or testing of the entire system at least every six months.	__	__	_____
The number of false alarms is kept below two for any six-month period.	__	__	_____
Upon alarm activation, there is a trained, armed person on the site within 20 minutes.	__	__	_____
Responsible members of the community living near the school have been requested to call the police if the alarm bell is heard.	__	__	_____
There is always someone available with keys to the school and alarm when the alarm is activated.	__	__	_____

	Yes	No	If No, Explain
Suitable procedures are established for turning the system on and off.	___	___	_____
High-risk areas are protected (e.g., office, cafeteria, shops, laboratories, music rooms, etc.).	___	___	_____
Selected areas of the school can be used while the remaining areas of the school are protected.	___	___	_____
There is back-up power to keep the system operating without generating an alarm if public power fails.	___	___	_____
Staff members are trained on the capabilities and limitations of the alarm system.	___	___	_____
Staff members are trained regarding their responsibilities when responding to an alarm.	___	___	_____

Frequency of Security and Safety Maintenance Checklist*

Purpose: This checklist is to help you establish the frequency with which the various security maintenance actions occur.

Directions: Check the line that indicates the frequency with which each item occurs. Enter the name of the individual responsible for conducting the check.

	Daily	Weekly	Monthly	6 Mo.	Annual	Whose Responsibility?
1a. Doors are checked to be certain they are secure.	____	____	____	____	____	_____
1b. Doors are checked to be certain they are in good working order.	____	____	____	____	____	_____
2a. Windows are checked to be certain they are secure.	____	____	____	____	____	_____
2b. Windows are checked to be certain they are in good working order.	____	____	____	____	____	_____
3. Outbuildings, storage sheds, portable classrooms and other school facilities are checked to be certain they are secure.	____	____	____	____	____	_____
4a. Fences and gates are checked to be certain they are secure.	____	____	____	____	____	_____
4b. Fences and gates are checked to be certain they are in proper working order.	____	____	____	____	____	_____
5. Lights are checked to be certain they are working properly.	____	____	____	____	____	_____
6. Fixtures are checked to be certain they are working properly.	____	____	____	____	____	_____
7. Playgrounds are checked to be certain that equipment is in working order.	____	____	____	____	____	_____

Risk Management Checklist

Safety Master Plan

__ Has a safety master plan been developed that addresses changing federal, state, and local rules, regulations, procedures, laws, codes, and maintenance requirements regarding school safety both within and in close proximity to the school site?

__ Is there documented evidence that safety regulations have in fact been met?

__ Does the safety master plan require posting specific sections that may include:

    __ charts or maps of fire alarms and extinguishing equipment

    __ maps of escape routes and fire/disaster relocation sites

    __ accessible telephones or other communication equipment

    __ utility valves and/or cut-offs

    __ basic first aid procedures

    __ phone numbers and addresses of community service agencies

    __ procedures for ensuring classroom and school safety

    __ posted behavior expectations

    __ school codes of conduct distributed and explained to students and parents

Board Policies

__ Have established school safety procedures, previously approved by the board of education or administrative personnel, been reviewed annually to ensure that all staff (certified, classified, part-time, and substitutes) know and understand safety procedures within their sphere of responsibility?

__ During this review process, have new concerns created by new programs or circumstances been formally recognized?

__ Has a policy of mitigation been approved by the board/administration, and have the appropriate personnel been informed and/or trained to meet the new concern?

Needs Assessment

__ Has a school safety needs assessment been completed by administration, teachers, students, parents, and interested community individuals to address the unique local safety needs of individuals coming into contact with the school (both in and out of session)?

School Safety

__ Is there an established procedure for ensuring the safety of teachers and students in the classroom? In hallways? On playgrounds or athletic fields? On field trips?

Visitors

__ Is there an established school visitor policy and is it posted?

__ Do staff "challenge" outsiders?

Maintenance

__ Is there an established maintenance schedule that is periodically checked by administrative personnel to ensure that the school site remains hazard-free?

Counseling

__ Are there counseling support personnel on campus, and are these personnel accessible to students at all times during the school day?

__ What conflict resolution techniques are available to students and/or staff?

Lighting

__ In addition to normal security lighting, is there adequate night lighting for programs or events that may take place after dark on school grounds?

__ Are there posted rules for maintaining a safe climate during extracurricular events, and are there security personnel to enforce those rules?

Food Service

__ Are there documented food preparation standards approved by state or local health agencies?

__ Are annual water tests, including tests for municipal water systems, conducted on site and approved in writing by an independent laboratory?

Hazardous Materials

__Is there documented evidence that hazardous materials (or equipment having reasonable potential for harming a student) have been periodically checked for the continued safety and maintenance of such items?

Medical

__ Are there qualified medical personnel on campus, and/or is there an established procedure for medical treatment or emergency transport of injured staff or students?

Crime and Violence

__ Is there an established policy for handling criminal acts by students or adults on campus?

__ What relationship exists with the local courts, probation office, and law enforcement?

Theft Prevention

__ Are school properties adequately marked and are expensive items properly stored to prevent theft or burglary?

Public Relations

__ Is there an ongoing public relations plan to communicate the school administration's goals and objectives to the staff, the community, and the media?

__ Is there a "crisis communications" plan to effectively deal with the media when problems arise?

Weapons Checklist*

Purpose: The Weapons Checklist contains elements to consider when the school decides to establish a school policy on firearms and possession of other weapons.

Directions: Check the line that best represents the school's current policy status on firearms and weapons possession. Use this information as input into your school's staff discussion on prioritizing needs for school improvement.

	Yes	No	In process
1. School policies are widely publicized.	___	___	___
2. School policies clearly define objects considered to be weapons.	___	___	___
3. School policies on weapons possession and searches are included in the Student Code of Conduct.	___	___	___
4. School policies provide for confiscation of any item considered to be a weapon.	___	___	___
5. School policies provide for notification of law enforcement and proper disposal of confiscated weapons.	___	___	___
6. School policies provide for reporting suspected or actual possession of weapons to school administrators.	___	___	___
7. School policies provide for searching students suspected of weapons violations.	___	___	___
8. School policies provide for suspension and/or expulsion of students for weapons violations.	___	___	___
9. School policies clearly state that it is illegal to possess a firearm in a school zone and that the individual will be arrested.	___	___	___
10. Staff training is provided in weapons detection, reporting, confiscation, and in confrontation when weapons are involved.	___	___	___
11. Weapons violations (including assaults with weapons) are reported to law enforcement.	___	___	___
12. A weapon crisis intervention and follow-up plan is in place.	___	___	___
13. Teachers and staff are trained on the weapons policy every _____.			

*Questions 1–7 and 9 are adapted from the *School Safety Checklist*, South Carolina Department of Education, December 1990, pp. 3–4.

Youth Gangs Checklist*

Purpose: The Youth Gangs Checklist contains items to be considered in assessing the school's current prevention strategies for dealing with gangs and gang-related activities.

Directions: Check the line that best represents the school's current status on the issue of youth gangs. Use this information as input in the school's discussion about how to effectively deal with gangs and gang-related activities.

	Yes	No	In Process
1. School policies clearly state that no gang insignias or clothing are allowed on campus.	___	___	___
2. The policy and consequences of item 1 are clearly outlined in the Student Code of Conduct.	___	___	___
3. The principal meets with gang members to inform them that gang-related activities will not be tolerated on or around school property.	___	___	___
4. Meetings with parent groups are held to discuss signs and symptoms of gang behavior and ways to discourage children from gang involvement and activity.	___	___	___
5. School staff are trained in identifying signs (including clothing) and symptoms of gang involvement and activity.	___	___	___
6. Law enforcement is notified by school officials of potential violence between gangs which may transpire before, during, or after school.	___	___	___
7. School staff assist law enforcement authorities in the identification of gang members and gangs operating in the community.	___	___	___

8. Gang identification training sessions for teachers are conducted every _____.

9. Gang identification training sessions for parents are conducted every _____.

10. School staff and law enforcement authorities meet to discuss gangs and gang-related problems every _____.

*Questions 1 and 2 are from the *School Safety Checkbook*, National School Safety Center, August 1990, p. 128; Questions 3–7 are from the *School Safety Checklist*, South Carolina Department of Education, December 1990, p. 3.

Transportation Safety Checklist*

Purpose: This Transportation Safety Checklist provides a series of items to aid in assessing the school's policies and provisions for school-sponsored transportation safety.

Directions: Check the line that best represents the current status of transportation safety at your school. Use this information as input into your school's discussion on prioritizing needs for school improvement.

	Yes	No	In Process
1. School bus safety rules have been developed and distributed to all students.	—	—	—
2. Parents have been informed in writing of school bus safety rules.	—	—	—
3. All students participate in school bus emergency evacuation drills twice annually.	—	—	—
4. Safety training is provided for all school bus drivers.	—	—	—
5. Drivers are trained in school bus discipline policies and procedures.	—	—	—
6. School bus routes are reviewed for hazardous conditions each year.	—	—	—
7. Passenger lists for all bus routes are maintained at the school site and are updated as changes occur.	—	—	—
8. School bus drivers maintain regular routes and schedules, and are on time for pickup before and after school.	—	—	—
9. Route descriptions for field trips are filed in the school office before trips begin.	—	—	—
10. Passenger lists are developed and filed in the school office for each vehicle used for a field trip.	—	—	—
11. All students and staff participating in a field trip are required to carry identification on their person.	—	—	—
12. Students with medical problems have identification of these problems on their person when participating in field trips.	—	—	—
13. Clear guidelines are established for chaperones for field trips, and these are communicated to all chaperones.	—	—	—
14. Accident procedures have been developed and communicated to bus drivers.	—	—	—

*Questions 1–7, 9–12 and 14 are from the *School Safety Checklist*, South Carolina Department of Education, December 1990, p. 7.

	Yes	No	In Process

15. Use of seat belts is required for all transportation performed in vehicles equipped with seat belts, if such transportation is school- or district-sponsored and/or approved. ___ ___ ___

16. Two-way communication is possible from all buses in case of emergency. ___ ___ ___

17. Bus drivers report student violations of school bus policy to administrators, and appropriate action is taken. ___ ___ ___

18. Incidents on buses and other school-sponsored transportation are included in the Incident Reporting System. ___ ___ ___

19. Bus drivers are notified when students on their buses are suspended or expelled. ___ ___ ___

20. Bus safety rules are reviewed and updated every _____.

21. Bus safety rules are communicated to students every _____.

22. Bus safety rules are communicated to parents every _____.

23. Bus drivers are provided training in safety and school discipline policies every _____.

24. Driving records of school bus drivers are reviewed/evaluated every _____.**

**State Board rule requires reviews in August, December, and during summer school.

Field Trip Checklist

Before a field trip, the following checklist items should be considered. Districtwide policies and procedures should be developed to address each of the questions in this checklist.

1. Has a clear educational purpose been established for the trip?
2. Have the program planners described where the group will go, how they will get there, who will supervise, when the group will arrive, when the group will leave, and how they may be contacted in an emergency?
3. Have parental/guardian release forms been obtained?
4. Have rules and regulations for student conduct on the field trip been established and communicated to students and parents/guardians in advance of the trip?
5. Is there a roster of all participating children and adults? Has each teacher been instructed to bring the class roster with him or her? Has a specific individual been assigned to maintain the participant roster?
6. Has emergency medical information been gathered on each student, staff member, and adult volunteer? Has someone been assigned to keep track of medical information and release forms in case of an emergency?
7. Have identification badges been made for all district and school staff who are involved in supervising students? Does each student have a student ID card or visible name badge? Has someone been appointed to ensure that ID badges are worn by all supervising personnel?
8. Has someone been assigned to be in charge of each event? Is there a clear chain of command to reporting or handling field trip emergencies?
9. If school vehicles are used for the field trip, what supervision will be provided on the vehicles?
10. Has a route plan been filed with the school? Is there a list of emergency medical facilities and emergency phone numbers within the vicinity or along the route the field trip will take?
11. Are bus drivers properly licensed and trained for the vehicle they will be driving? In addition, have the drivers received appropriate training in emergency procedures?
12. If private cars are used to transport students, has the district been provided with certificates of insurance confirming that the vehicles and their drivers are properly insured?
13. Have background checks on adult volunteers been completed to ensure that there are no child molesters or known felons volunteering to supervise students?
14. Have adequate steps been taken to ensure that there is a reasonable ratio of adults to students?
15. Do supervising personnel have CPR or emergency medical training?
16. Should a certified school nurse go on the field trip, based upon the size of the group and the destination?
17. If the field trip is a beach or water outing, will there be adequate life guarding staff whose certifications are current?
18. Are an emergency first-aid kit, bull horn, and flashlight available for the trip?
19. Is there radio communication or cellular phone capability?
20. What arrangements have been made for parents or guardians to pick up students after the field trip?

Sample Plans, Policies, Procedures, and Codes

Comprehensive Plan for Safe and Secure Campuses 135
Oakland Unified School District, Oakland, California

Model School Safety Plan 143
Kentucky School Board Association

Safety and Health Functions 145
Hawaii Department of Education

Guidelines for Student Behavior 147
San Leandro Unified School District, San Leandro, California

Chancellor's Regulation on Carrying Weapons in School 149
City School District of the City of New York

Anti-Gang and Drug Policy and Procedures 151
San Bernardino City Unified School District, California

Dress Code 157
Las Virgenes Unified School District, Calabasas, California

OAKLAND UNIFIED SCHOOL DISTRICT
Office of the Superintendent

January 22, 1992

TO: Board of Education

FROM: Richard P. Mesa, Superintendent

RE: Comprehensive Plan for Safe and Secure Campuses

INTRODUCTION

Article 1, section 28(c) of the California Constitution states that "all students and staff of public primary, elementary, junior high and senior high schools have the inalienable right to attend campuses which are safe, secure and peaceful." The Oakland Unified School district (OUSD) is legally and morally responsible for the establishment of policy which ensures that schools are free from violence, threats of violence, and the use or sale of dangerous and illegal drugs or other disruptive behavior by individuals or groups.

Accomplishing this task presents serious challenges to the district. Oakland's schools do not exist in a vacuum; instead, they operate in a society in which violence, including the use of deadly force, has become a common way of resolving problems and disputes of every kind. Although the district would prefer that its schools were sanctuaries from the troubles of the outside world, they are instead a continuation of it. Far from being unique among American cities, Oakland is typical of urban areas plagued by drug abuse, crime, and violence. Although a very small percentage of the district's students actually engage in violence or other illegal conduct, all are threatened by it. Most incidents of serious violence which occur on the district's campuses result from off-campus disputes which are carried across school boundaries. A large number of such incidents result from the actions of persons who are not OUSD students.

The district's Five Year Educational Plan articulates a series of student outcomes whose achievement will demonstrate the success of the district's mission statement. The plan recognizes that those outcomes can be achieved only if we are successful in creating district, school, and classroom conditions that are consistent with the outcomes. Several of those conditions may be paraphrased as follows:

1. School and classroom climates are safe and secure, providing conditions which help students affiliate with their peers and feel equally valued.

2. Students' life circumstances are identified, incorporated into, and addressed by district and school policies. Resources are distributed equitably to address life circumstances.

3. Home and school interaction is collaborative, and all parents are ascribed equal status, welcomed, and involved in the education of their children.

4. Students receive extra support to learn the academic and personal skills to succeed.

Unsafe conditions in our communities create serious difficulties in establishing these conditions. Violence in Oakland continues at an alarming rate, and people wonder whether this year's homicide total will be slightly less than or exceed the record of 1990.

At the same time our schools must deal with children whose families are plagued by substance abuse, homelessness, inadequate nutrition, and often nonexistent health care. Put simply, many children lack not only the support they need to succeed in school, but must also cope with problems which make learning and school attendance problematic, to say the least.

In this context it is important for the district to establish a comprehensive strategy to deal with the problems posed by violence in our community and students' life circumstances. As always, the district is severely constrained by inadequate resources. At the same time it is necessary to perform a balancing act, attempting to deal with the almost daily crises caused by community violence while addressing the chronic conditions which impact students' life circumstances and affect their education.

The purpose of the Comprehensive Health and Safety Plan is to ensure to the extent possible that our campuses are safe in the immediate future and that they are places where guns, violence, and criminal activity are effectively barred. At the same time that we create space for teaching and learning, we must build into our structure programs which address the causes of violence, assist young people at risk of falling into violent pathologies, and help all students develop the skills necessary to confront and deal with life's crises without resorting to violence.

SUMMARY

The interventions listed below — including violence prevention curriculum, alternative schools, drug education, school climate, and security measures — represent our responses to violence. They range, first, through immediate and direct actions; second, through intermediate interventions aimed at changing student attitudes to prevent violence; and third, longer term interventions to address the causes of the violence and threats that plague our schools.

Immediate and Direct Actions to Keep Weapons Out of the Schools

I.   The plan includes immediate and direct actions to eliminate weapons, especially guns, from campuses and to prevent or stop physical assaults, reduce the incidents of fighting, rout out the intimidation, extortion, and other victimization of some students by others and to prevent or stop immediate threats of gang conflict.

   A.   Enclose schools with intrusion-proof fencing.
   B.   Close campuses.
   C.   Provide IDs for students.
   D.   Use metal detectors as necessary.
   E.   Assign sufficient number of campus supervisors to prevent or respond to problems quickly.
   F.   Team with the city police to provide quick police response.

Strategies to Change Student Attitudes and Behaviors and Improve School Climate

II.   The plan also includes strategies that take longer to affect students' attitudes and other causes of violence. Many of these interventions are operating in the district already and will require expansion to the sites that need them.

A. Conflict mediation.
B. Teens on Target.
C. Violence prevention curriculum.
D. Discover Skills for Life.
E. Alternative schools.
F. Social case work managers and elementary school counselors.
G. SB 65 program.
H. Dress code.
I. Parents' presence and mentoring.
J. Teen Centers.

Addressing the Root Causes of Violence and Weapons Use

III. This third category of interventions is aimed at routing out the causes of student abuse and violence. This is not a complete list, but it does identify the more important efforts needed.

A. Classroom and School Interventions
1. Staff development to educate teachers to develop positive student-teacher interactions.
2. Curriculum that elicits student interaction, involvement, and thinking.
3. Teaching methods that are interactive and motivating.
4. Multicultural curriculum that enhances personal and cross-cultural understanding and respect.

B. Environment
1. Cooperate with community and police efforts to reduce crime, violence, and drugs in our neighborhoods.
2. Through mentors and tutors, provide adult contact, especially male role models.
3. Provide parent education to control excessive television viewing, especially of violence.
4. Cooperate with the city to reinstate recreation and other constructive after-school activities.
5. Eliminate inequity in schools and provide vocational education to increase job opportunities.
6. Coordinate community health, social welfare, jobs, and other services for families.
7. Increase pre-school and latchkey programs.

C. Home
1. Parent involvement.
2. Parent education.
3. Address life circumstances, such as homelessness, mobility, etc.
4. Coordinated services.

COMPREHENSIVE PLAN

I. This element of the plan involves securing our schools from outsiders who would disrupt them and from the alarming increase of weapons carried by students. In this context it is important to note that nationwide almost 20 percent of all students have reported that they carry weapons at least occasionally. In a recent study by the United States Department of Justice, three percent of students in central cities indicated that they had carried weapons to school at least once in the preceding six months.

A. Fences

Several schools in the district are extremely vulnerable to intrusion by outsiders because they occupy large areas of land which is either unfenced or imperfectly fenced. The district is exploring the costs of fencing such campuses in a secure, attractive way. It is the district's goal to provide such fencing on all campuses which require it so that access and egress may be controlled with a few campus supervisors. By early 1992 staff will prepare a proposed priority list and cost estimates for fencing campuses.

B. Closing Campuses

Presently all district high schools, with the exception of Skyline, are open, which means that students may leave during the lunch period. Many students leave, at lunch as well as at other times, and do not return. Likewise, having open campuses makes it difficult to determine whether a person entering the campus does or does not belong there. No later than September 1, 1992, all campuses will be closed during the school day. In order to prepare for this change, all affected campuses will have to improve their ability to provide meals to students and maintain security during the lunch hour.

C. Student Identification Cards

Many district schools, including Skyline and Montera, now issue identification cards to students. No later than September 1992, all secondary students will be provided with identification cards, and procedures will be developed to deal with issues of cost, display, and replacement of such cards.

D. Metal Detectors

The district will acquire hand-held metal detectors for periodic checks of students and their belongings. The district does not plan to make each student pass through a metal detector each day. Rather, the district believes that occasional, unannounced use of metal detectors by trained personnel who will respect students' rights will increase awareness of the risk of bringing a weapon onto a district campus.

E. Campus Supervisors

The district currently employs 108 campus supervisors who are assigned to school sites based primarily upon student population. Other factors may affect the allocation at schools with particular needs. By early 1992 we will create a "Special Response Team" in each area to add support in crisis situations. In addition, some school principals have indicated that they would prefer full-time police officers rather than part of their allotments of campus supervisors. This option is being explored, both from the perspective of the district's financial ability and the availability of sufficient officers. Campus supervisors will be supplemented by parent patrols at selected schools.

F. Police Services

The district's present police services staff consists of five officers, two sergeants, and a city police lieutenant who works with the district through a contract with the City of Oakland. Two additional offices have been hired and will graduate from the police academy in early 1992. The district's ratio of police officers is far less, for example, then that which exists in Los Angeles, where there is one officer for each 3,000 students. However, the city has recently committed to the assignment of six additional city officers to work with the district police services unit after the first of the year. This increased force will allow the district to assign two officers on a full-time basis to each comprehensive high school attendance area. This will make it possible, when necessary, to have an officer with a particular campus on virtually a full-time basis to deal with emergencies and help improve school climate.

II. Strategies to Change Student Attitudes and Behaviors and Improve School Climate

Banning weapons and intruders from our campuses will not be sufficient to ensure school safety. In addition, it is necessary to adopt and implement policies which will ensure that campuses are safe, peaceful, and harmonious places of learning.

Many Oakland students are "at risk" of becoming involved in antisocial behavior due to problems in their homes and/or communities. For such students it is critical that the district work in collaboration with other public and private agencies to address their life circumstances and to provide the support necessary to help them attend and be successful in school. The following district programs address these concerns. At this stage the programs must be described as experimental and fragmentary because they do not reach anywhere near the number of students who might benefit from them. A major effort must be made to increase the resources available for these programs. Much of these resources must come from funds outside the district's educational budget.

The district will work closely with other public entities to increase resources for such programs. We are involved in an ongoing discussion with the city and the county on a proposal to develop schools as multi-service community centers. The district, the city, and the Oakland Housing Authority are also developing a proposal for a model collaboration involving Havenscourt Junior High, Lockwood Elementary, and the Lockwood Gardens housing project, based upon a model in Dade County, Florida.

A. Conflict Resolution Programs

Conflict resolution programs have operated in the district for over five years at several high schools and are now in place at four senior and three junior high schools. In addition, conflict resolution programs exist at many elementary schools, and teachers are being trained in developing such programs at many others. The district believes that these programs greatly improve school climate by providing training to students in how to resolve their own disputes and by placing a positive value on such dispute resolution. The Board of Education has already allocated $100,000 to train elementary school teachers in conflict resolution techniques. The district will establish conflict resolution programs at all schools no later than September 1992.

B. Teens on Target

High school students, themselves at risk of becoming involved in antisocial behavior, have been trained in a number of issues including drugs, street and domestic violence, AIDS, and handgun prevention. As part of a class they develop videos on these issues and make presentations to high school and middle/junior high school students. This is an example of a program which utilizes mentors to assist students in making the correct decisions and avoiding certain kinds of behavior. The district will carefully evaluate this program and determine if it should be repeated next year.

C. Violence Prevention Curriculum

The district is now investigating a very promising curriculum developed by Dr. Deborah Prothrow-Stith, assistant dean of the Harvard School of Public Health. Her Violence Prevention Curriculum for Adolescents is presently being used in 400 schools in 45 states. The district will attempt to test this curriculum with tenth-grade students at several high schools beginning in September 1992.

D. Discover Skills for Life

The district is presently testing the Discover Skills for Life program at 13 target elementary and middle/junior high schools. This is the program's second year of implementation. It provides a comprehensive approach involving substance abuse and life skills and is one of the programs being utilized statewide in an effort to develop a uniform California health curriculum.

E. Alternative Schools

The district will research various models of alternative secondary schools which can be developed to meet the needs of students who are not succeeding in the regular schools. Such programs must include the following components: challenging and comprehensive curriculum, relevant job training, comprehensive support services, and a safe, secure environment. Plans are currently under way to further develop the program at Dewey Continuation High School in accordance with these criteria. In addition, staff are developing plans for a new alternative school to serve junior high school age students beginning in September 1992.

F. Social Work Case Management

This program is provided at 13 schools — Santa Fe, Hoover, Cox, Webster, Whittier, Lockwood, Lowell, Carter, Simmons, Havenscourt, Frick, Elmhurst, and Madison — and is funded with $644,000 of the district's grant from the state's Drug, Alcohol, and Tobacco ("DATE") funds. The purpose of this program is (1) to coordinate services among various social welfare, educational, and criminal justice system agencies which provide services to a student and his or her family; and (2) to provide individual, group, and family counseling, crisis intervention, and home visitation. The goal of this program is to remediate conditions which lead to antisocial behavior and school failure. Services are provided by several agencies: Asian Community Mental Health, East Bay Activity Center, East Oakland Youth Development Center, Oakland Community Counseling, West Oakland Health Counsel, and Xanthos. A preliminary evaluation of this program conducted by the Child Welfare Research Center at the School of Social Welfare, University of California at Berkeley, found that it was relatively successful during its year of operation and is a "pioneering project" which has "moved beyond conceptualization and rhetoric and is now engaged in the difficult challenge of changing the way that community agencies and the schools do business."

G. SB 65 Program

This state Department of Education program represents a focused effort to reduce truancy at 12 schools. The SB 65 workers assist district staff in developing programs which outreach to truant students and their families, coordinate and provide support services, and provide staff development to site employees.

H. Dress Code

The Board of Education has already adopted a dress code, which will be implemented beginning the second semester in January 1992. The dress code will ensure that students are not intimidated by other students who wear gang clothing or insignia. It will also facilitate the wearing of uniforms at some schools and discourage students from wearing items which become the cause of fights or robberies. Enforcement of the dress code will decrease the influence of gangs at our schools.

I. Parent Involvement

The Board of Education has already approved in principle a proposal to employ staff to increase parent involvement in our schools. The district believes that having more adults on our campuses, with the ultimate goal of having an adult in almost every classroom, will create an atmosphere where good behavior is expected and encouraged.

J. Teen Centers

The Westlake Teen Center provides after-school activities including academic support, conflict mediation, and cultural awareness. These activities improve school climate by helping students understand and appreciate each other. The district will evaluate this program and attempt to replicate it at other schools beginning September 1992.

III. Addressing the Root Causes of Violence and Weapons Use

Over the long term the most important thing that the district can do to improve school safety and security will be to train students in the skills and behavior necessary to avoid dangerous and antisocial conduct and to adopt healthy lifestyles including nonviolent, constructive approaches to problem solving. The district has begun to implement such a curriculum, but much more needs to be done to improve these efforts and to integrate them with the district's core educational program.

A. Community Drug-Free School Zones Project

The district has obtained a $900,000, three-year grant from the State Department of Alcohol and Drug Programs to assist the students at Castlemont High School in several ways. The funds from this program are being used for job training and counseling, a teen parenting program, social case work management, parent liaisons, and increased security in the form of parent patrols.

B. DARE Program

The Oakland Police Department has assigned eight police officers to teach the DARE drug and high-risk behavior prevention program at all district elementary schools. This program, which is utilized nationally, is now an established facet of collaboration between the district and the city.

C. Parent and Grandparent Support

This pilot program at Webster Academy and Cox Elementary is funded through the district's DATE grant. It provides outreach to parents, grandparents, and other care givers to create closer home-school collaboration, provide assistance in development of parenting skills and support for students, and improve school climate.

D. After-School Math and Tutorial Program

Funded through DATE and Chapter I funds, after-school tutoring and enrichment programs are provided at five elementary schools: Stonehurst, Cox, Webster, Whittier, and Lockwood. A major component of the district's Five Year Educational Plan is to provide tutoring and mentoring to students throughout the district. The evaluation of this existing program will provide us with lessons needed to expand and improve tutorial services.

E. Oakland Police Athletic League

The Oakland Police Athletic League funds and staffs an after-school enrichment program at Madison Middle School. Full-time police officers and volunteers provide recreation, tutoring, and mentoring during afternoons and early evenings. This program is being expanded to provide additional support to the students at Madison Middle School.

DS:cr
003.BMC92

Model School Safety Plan
Kentucky School Board Association

I. Introduction

II. School Safety Assessment

A. What instrument do you use to assess your school climate, student behavior and attitudes? How are results evaluated and utilized?

B. How do you identify students who might be at risk in terms of their safety or the safety of others?

C. What opportunities are students given to provide staff with feedback about school environment?

D. What system of referral exists to meet the needs of students identified as potentially at risk?

III. Facilities Safety Assessment

A. What security devices are necessary and exist in your building? (metal detectors, classroom telephones, etc.)

B. Does a clear, up-to-date floor plan of your school exist? Who has it?

C. Have unsafe areas been identified? What long-range plans have been made to eliminate potential dangers?

D. Where do visitors enter the building?

E. How effective is the school's communication system — within the school, with community agencies, with transportation staff?

IV. School Discipline Assessment

A. Is your code of student discipline simply and clearly written?

B. How effective is the code? How effectively is it enforced?

C. Do you have a student sign-out process which promotes student safety? Is it consistently enforced?

D. What process do you have to assess and monitor the progress of juvenile offenders returned to school?

E. Is the focus of your discipline code the safety of non-offending students?

V. Alternative Education Assessment

A. Do you identify all students who could possibly become at risk for dangerous behaviors?

B. What services are provided to address the needs of these individual students?

C. What processes exist to remove potentially dangerous students from the regular student body?

D. What is the selection process for alternative education programs? How do students enter and leave? What is the rate of success for these programs?

E. Are alternative education programs active, innovative research-based intervention rather than simply "holding tanks"?

F. Is there community, district, and state support for your alternative programs?

VI. Community and Parent Involvement Assessment

A. How do you communicate school safety issues to the public?

B. Do you communicate your discipline code to the public?

C. What is done to encourage parent accountability?

D. How are parents involved early in the student discipline process?

E. How do you use local media to inform the community about school safety, student discipline, and intervention programs?

F. How do you educate parents about their responsibilities?

G. How do you utilize and cooperate with local community resource agencies?

H. How do you share common safety issues and solutions with local businesses?

I. How do you share related professional development opportunities with parents and community partners?

VII. Crisis Management Assessment

A. What specific plan do you have to handle a crisis situation? How is it communicated to staff and students?

B. What plan governs media contact in a potential crisis? Who is the designated spokesperson?

C. Does each school staff person know his or her role in a crisis? What training have they received?

D. Is there a crisis response team on site? In the district?

E. Which staff members have received first-aid training? How are they identified for staff and students?

F. Is the staff well trained in crisis management?

G. Do you have a list of community and state resource contacts? Where is it posted?

Safety and Health Functions
Hawaii Department of Education

The Hawaii Department of Education has placed safety and health functions into three broad categories — workplace safety, employee safety, and student safety. The following table delineates which functions are to be managed by three systemwide support offices. This table illustrates the many components of safe school planning, many of which should be addressed by the safe schools team.

Schools, through their district office, can seek assistance from the following support offices for safety- and health-related issues.

Office of Business Services (Workplace Safety)

- Asbestos
- Bomb Threat
- Breakfast and Lunch Supervision: Safety and Control
- Burglaries, Theft, Fire and Vandalism Procedures
- Cafeteria Dining Room: Health Sanitation and Safety
- Closing of School
- Custodial Safety Concerns
- Electric and Magnetic Fields (EMF)
- Emergency Preparedness (Civil Defense)
- Facilities Safety Design Concerns
- Hazard Communication
- Hazardous Materials (Chemicals) Episodes (Spills)
- Hazardous Materials Storage and Disposal Coordination
- Helicopter Landings at Schools
- HIOSH Regulations
- HIOSH Regulations Interpretation
- Indoor Air Quality
- Intrusion Alarm Activation
- Junior Police Officers Safety
- Lead in Paint Concerns
- Lead in School's Drinking Water
- Night Security Concerns
- OSHA 200
- Radon
- Reasonable Use of Force
- School Fire Inspection Concerns
- School Inspection Program Concerns
- School Security Attendants
- Student Accidents: Form 411
- Student Transportation
- Tobacco-Free Schools, Administrative Rule, Chapter 31
- Tort Claim: Personal Injury/ Property Damage
- Traffic Safety
- Use of Private Vehicles to Transport Students

Office of Personnel Services (Employee Safety)

- Access to Telephone after Work Hours
- Blood-Borne Pathogens Exposure Control Plan
- Cafeteria Safety and Sanitation Concerns
- Claims for Legislative Relief
- Compliance with Applicable Federal, State and Local Safety Laws, Rules and Regulations
- Drug-Free Schools
- Employee Accident Reporting
- Lighting and Ventilation
- Motor Vehicle
- Payment for Medical, Surgical and Hospital Services
- Protection against Inclement Weather
- Protection against Threats or Violence/Security
- Protective Clothing/Safety Equipment Tools
- Provisions of Adequate and Sanitary Toilet and Washing Facilities and Drinking Water
- Reimbursement for Personal Clothing, Prescription Glasses and Watches
- Removal of Any Known Unauthorized Persons from School Campuses
- Renovation/Construction Provisions
- Safety Committees
- Student Discipline
- Student Medication
- Teacher Assault and Administrative Assistance
- Temporary Hazard Pay
- Visitation by Non-School Personnel or Students not Enrolled in that School

Office of Instructional Services (Student Safety)

- Alcohol, Tobacco, and Other Drug Use, Possession, or Sale
- Art Education, Arts and Crafts, Art Safety
- Artist-in-the-Schools/Performing and Visual Arts
- Bicycle Safety
- Campus Disturbance Plan
- Chapter 19
- Driver Education Reporting Accidents
- Field Trips
- Health Education Curriculum
- Interscholastic Athletics Program
- Playground Safety (Equipment)
- Practical Arts and Vocational and Applied Technology Education
- Project Prom/Graduation: A Traffic Safety and Alcohol/Drug-Free Activity
- Safety and Security Plan for Athletic Events
- School Health Services
- School Safety Planning (General)
- Science Laboratory
- Student Travel/Field Trips
- Water-related Student Activities
- Youth Gang Concerns

GUIDELINES FOR STUDENT BEHAVIOR

PROBLEM AREAS

TARDINESS
Arriving late to class

UNEXCUSED ABSENCE AND CUTTING
Any absence which has not been both excused by a parent or legal guardian and approved by the appropriate school official.

DEFIANCE OF SCHOOL PERSONNEL'S AUTHORITY
Refusal to comply with reasonable requests of school personnel.

DISORDERLY CONDUCT, INCLUDING PROFANITY AND OBSCENE BEHAVIOR
Conduct and/or behavior which is disruptive to the orderly educational procedure of the school including habitual profanity or vulbarity.

DRESS CODE
Failure to observe the school's dress code.

BUS
Not following bus safety rules.

VERBAL ABUSE
Statements which intimidate or injure another person.

FORGERY
Using signature or initials of a teacher, or parent.

THEFT
Receiving, attempting or taking property that doesn't belong to you.

SMOKING/TOBACCO POSSESSION
The use or possession of tobacco, of any kind, on school property or at school activities.

DESTRUCTION OR DEFACEMENT OF PROPERTY
Attempting to damage, destroy or mutilate objects or materials belonging to the school, school personnel, or other persons.

FIGHTING
Engaging in or threatening physical contact for the purpose of inflicting harm or another person.

*ARSON
Intentional burning of property.

*ALCOHOL
The use, possession, or sale of alcoholic substances.

*DRUGS
Possession of drug paraphernalia, sale, furnishing or use of controlled substances or their look-alikes.

*PHYSICAL ASSAULT
Physical attack of one person, or of a group of persons, upon another person who does not wish to engage in the conflict.

*WEAPONS
The use, possession or furnishing of any knife, firearm, or other dangerous object.

*EXTORTION/ROBBERY
The solicitation of money, or something of value, from another person, in return for protection, or in connection with a threat to inflict harm or robbing a person.

*EXPLOSIVE DEVICES
The use, possession or sale of explosive device.

*Expulsion may occur on first offense.

DISCIPLINARY ACTIONS

Students who become involved in areas of problem behavior will be subject to certain disciplinary actions. Depending upon the behavior problem of the student, one or more of the following actions may be taken by the school officials. The action taken will be according to Board policies and State law.

INFORMAL TALK A school official (teacher, administrator or counselor) will talk to the student and try to reach an agreement regarding how the student should behave. Recorded in Administrative record.

CONFERENCE A formal conference is held between the student and one or more school officials. During this conference, the student must agree to correct his/her behavior. Recorded in Administrative record.

DETENTION Students may be detained in school for disciplinary or other reasons for a maximum of 1 hour after the close of the school day.

WEEKEND SCHOOL Students may be assigned to school on weekends in lieu of more serious disciplinary action.

SARB - School Attendance Review Board

REMOVING FROM CLASSES The student is removed from one or more classes, but remains at school during these class periods, or receives appropriate disciplinary action such as: (1) serves one or more detention work details; (2) has privileges suspended; (3) has privileges suspended. Recorded in Student File; (4) removed from class for semester.

IN-SCHOOL SUSPENSION A student may be assigned to an in-school suspension program at the discretion of the principal or designee for offenses for which suspension is permitted.

SUSPENSION The student is informed that he/she is subject to a suspension (five days or less). The student is also informed regarding the due process procedure. The student's parent(s) or legal guardian is notified by telephone that the student is subject to a suspension. Notification to the parent(s) or legal guardian must include clear instructions regarding the due process procedure. Recorded in student record.

TRANSFER TO CONTINUATION/OPPORTUNITY SCHOOL A proposed involuntary transfer notice may be sent to the parent/guardian to initiate the transfer for the student to receive special behavioral and educational services. Parents/students have an opportunity to appeal per Board Policy.

SEMESTER SUSPENSION A continuation student may receive a semester suspension for a violation of the district discipline policy.

EXPULSION The student is informed that he/she is subject to expulsion. the student is also informed regarding the due process procedure. The student's parent(s) or legal guardian is notified by telephone and certified letter that the student is subject to expulsion. Notification to the parent(s) or legal guardian must include clear instructions regarding the due process procedure. The school district superintendent will recommend to the Board of Education that the student be expelled. The due process procedure is immediately initiated. The expulsion does not become effective until the due process procedure has been completed. Recorded in Student File.

RELATIONSHIP BETWEEN PROBLEM AREA & DISCIPLINARY ACTION

PROBLEM AREAS	RANGE	POSSIBLE ACTIONS TO BE TAKEN FIRST OCCURRENCE	REPEATED OCCURRENCES
TARDINESS	MINIMUM	INFORMAL TALK	PARENT INVOLVEMENT
	MAXIMUM	DETENTION	DROP FROM CLASS
UNEXCUSED ABSENCE	MINIMUM	PARENT NOTICE	WEEKEND CLASS/DETENTION
	MAXIMUM	SARB	CONTINUATION/OPPORTUNITY
DEFIANCE OF AUTHORITY	MINIMUM	CONFERENCE	PARENT INVOLVEMENT
	MAXIMUM	SUSPENSION	CONTINUATION/OPPORTUNITY
DISORDERLY CONDUCT	MINIMUM	INFORMAL TALK	PARENT INVOLVEMENT
	MAXIMUM	SUSPENSION	CONTINUATION/OPPORTUNITY
DRESS CODE	MINIMUM	INFORMAL TALK	CONFERENCE
	MAXIMUM	SUSPENSION	
VERBAL ABUSE	MINIMUM	INFORMAL TALK	CONFERENCE
	MAXIMUM	SUSPENSION	
FORGERY	MINIMUM	PARENT INVOLVEMENT	
	MAXIMUM	SUSPENSION	
THEFT	MINIMUM	PARENT INVOLVEMENT	
	MAXIMUM	SUSPENSION	EXPULSION
SMOKING	MINIMUM	PARENT INVOLVEMENT	SUSPENSION
	MAXIMUM	SUSPENSION	CONTINUATION/OPPORTUNITY

PROBLEM AREAS	RANGE	POSSIBLE ACTIONS TO BE TAKEN FIRST OCCURRENCE	REPEATED OCCURRENCES
DESTRUCTION OF PROPERTY	MINIMUM	PARENT INVOLVEMENT	
	MAXIMUM	SUSPENSION	EXPULSION
FIGHTING	MINIMUM	PARENT INVOLVEMENT	
	MAXIMUM	SUSPENSION	EXPULSION
ALCOHOL	MINIMUM	SUSPENSION	SUSPENSION
	MAXIMUM	CONTINUATION/OPPORTUNITY	EXPULSION
*PHYSICAL ASSAULT	MINIMUM	SUSPENSION	SUSPENSION
	MAXIMUM	EXPULSION	EXPULSION
*ARSON	MINIMUM	SUSPENSION	SUSPENSION
	MAXIMUM	EXPULSION	EXPULSION
*DRUGS	MINIMUM	SUSPENSION	SUSPENSION
	MAXIMUM	EXPULSION	EXPULSION
*WEAPONS	MINIMUM	SUSPENSION	SUSPENSION
	MAXIMUM	EXPULSION	EXPULSION
*EXTORTION/ROBBERY	MINIMUM	SUSPENSION	SUSPENSION
	MAXIMUM	EXPULSION	EXPULSION
*EXPLOSIVE DEVICES	MINIMUM	SUSPENSION	SUSPENSION
	MAXIMUM	EXPULSION	EXPULSION

This chart has explained the major disciplinary problem areas and the actions that may result for those students who cannot live by the rules. All students are entitled to due process. This means there are certain procedures which school officials will follow prior to taking appropriate disciplinary action. There are also procedures which students must follow, if they do not agree with the school's actions.

Hopefully, students will never be in a situation where they need the protection of due process. If, however, a student does become involved in a situation in which a suspension or expulsion might result, both the student and his/her parents will be given a more detailed description of the due process procedures. The following summary is only to acquaint students and parents that such a procedure exists.

YOUR RIGHTS - DUE PROCESS

SUSPENSIONS AND EXPULSIONS

• The school principal or designee has the right to suspend a student for a period of up to five days. In cases of this type, an informal hearing between the principal, student, and other appropriate persons will be conducted if possible. After the hearing is completed, the principal decides if a suspension is necessary. The principal will attempt to notify parents by telephone before this action is taken. Students or parents may appeal. A written notice will be sent.

• The school principal has the right to recommend to the district superintendent that a student should be expelled. In cases of this type, a hearing will be conducted at the school district central office before the board hearing.

• When the school principal recommends to the district superintendent that a student should be expelled, the hearing will be conducted before the Board of Education or a hearing panel.

• If a student has violated a school rule and is subject to a suspension or transfer to Continuation/Opportunity school or expulsion, the student and his/her parents, guardians, will be formally notified. Part of the notification process will include instructions regarding the due process procedure.

APPEAL

• The student or the student's parents have the right to appeal a suspension or expulsion.

• An appeal for a formal hearing at either the district or Board of Education level, whichever is appropriate, must be made after notice has been received regarding a potential suspension, or transfer or expulsion.

SAN LEANDRO UNIFIED SCHOOL DISTRICT   SCHOOL _____

Chancellor's Regulation on Carrying Weapons in School
A-430, Students' Volume
Abstract
City School District of the City of New York

Any person carrying a weapon in a school building, facility, or contract vehicle used to transport students to and from school poses a clear and present danger to other students and staff and is subject to suspension by a superintendent or the executive director of the Division of Special Education, as well as possible criminal or juvenile delinquency prosecution. As used hereafter throughout this *Regulation*, the term "superintendent" indicates the executive director of the Division of Special Education or his designee in suspensions involving special education students as defined in *Regulation of the Chancellor* A-445, and in suspensions involving other students, the community, and the borough or assistant superintendent, as appropriate. *Regulation of the Chancellor* A-440, Suspension of Other Than High School Students, and *Regulation of the Chancellor* A-441, Suspension of High School Students, governs the suspension of students carrying weapons, except as otherwise provided in this *Regulation*.

I. Automatic Superintendent's Suspension and Summoning of Police

Possession of the following weapons will result in an automatic Superintendent's Suspension:

- Firearm (including a pistol, handgun, and any gun small enough to be concealed on the body), firearm silencer, and electronic dart gun;
- Shotgun, rifle, machine gun, or any other weapon that simulates or is adaptable for use as a machine gun;
- Switchblade knife, gravity knife, and cane sword (a cane that conceals a knife);
- Billy (club), blackjack, bludgeon, chucka stick, and metal knuckles;
- Sandbag and sandclub;
- Slungshot (small heavy weights attached to a thong);
- Explosive, incendiary bomb, and bombshell;
- Dagger, stiletto, dangerous knife, and straight razor; and
- Air gun, spring gun, or other instrument or weapon in which the propelling force is a spring or air, and any weapon in which any loaded or blank cartridge may be used (such as a BB gun).

Possession of any of these weapons is totally proscribed for all staff, students, and school visitors, and it constitutes grounds for criminal arrest, regardless of whether the weapon is loaded. A police officer is to be summoned for the purpose of making an arrest. The Bureau of School Safety is to be notified immediately, and all procedures described in *Regulation of the Chancellor* A-412 are to be followed.

II. Superintendent's Suspension and Summoning of Police at the Discretion of the Principal

Mere possession of certain other articles is forbidden and, under most circumstances, will result in a Superintendent's Suspension. The Bureau of School Safety is to be notified immediately, and all procedures described in *Regulation of the Chancellor* A-412 are to be followed.

Possession of the following articles is forbidden:
- Acid or other deadly or dangerous chemicals;
- Imitation pistol;
- Loaded or blank cartridges and ammunition; and
- Any deadly, dangerous, or sharp pointed instrument that can be used as a weapon (such as broken glass, case cutter, chains, wire).

Before invoking a suspension, the principal, in consultation with the Bureau of School Safety, shall consider whether or not there are mitigating factors involved in the possession of a particular article, for example, a nail file, for which a purpose exists other than infliction of physical or mental harm. However, when there are factors to indicate that an individual in possession of such an article has the intention of using it as a weapon in order to inflict physical or mental harm, the principal shall seek a Superintendent's Suspension and immediately summon the police for purposes of making an arrest.

III. Confiscation and Disposal of Weapons and Other Dangerous Articles

When a person is found to be in possession of a weapon or other dangerous article as described in Sections I and II of this *Regulation*, the principal, the school guard, or the police officer, depending on the circumstances, shall confiscate the article. In instances that do not require the police to be summoned, the article shall be given into the custody of the Bureau of School Safety.

Unless the police take custody of the weapon, the Bureau of School Safety shall retain its custody and when notified of the date of the suspension hearing, shall present the article as evidence in the hearing. Upon notice that a weapons case involving suspension has been decided by the superintendent, or upon notice that a weapons possession case will not entail a student suspension, the Bureau of School Safety shall dispose of confiscated articles by delivering them to the local police precinct.

IV. Authorization for Suspension for Possession of Weapons

At the request of the principal, the superintendent shall have emergency authority to invoke an automatic, emergency suspension of any student found to be in possession of any weapons described in Sections I and II of this *Regulation*. Any suspension for possession of weapons must be made by the superintendent. Principals' suspensions are not to be invoked in these cases.

Anti-Gang and Drug Policy and Procedures
San Bernardino City Unified School District, California

Introduction to Safe Schools

The Board of Education, sensing the urgency of the significant increase in gang activity near our schools, directed the superintendent and staff to provide safe school programs to ensure that all students, employees, and visiting community members are provided a safe learning and working environment.

To address this significant concern, we have worked closely with city and county government and their law enforcement agencies to provide programs to intervene as well as prevent this negative influence from affecting our schools. We have provided this brochure as a quick reference to these programs.

Please contact the persons listed for further information on any program. Your awareness of the problem and support of our efforts will result in better lives for the students we serve.

E. Neal Roberts, Ed.D.,　　　　　　　　*Herbert R. Fischer, Ph.D.,*
Superintendent　　　　　　　　　　　*Assistant Superintendent, Special Services*
S.B.C.U.S.D.　　　　　　　　　　　　*S.B.C.U.S.D.*

Look-Alike Weapons

In 1990 the San Bernardino City Unified School District Board of Education adopted a policy which is designed to assist school staffs in providing a safe learning and working environment. The policy prevents students from bringing onto school campuses objects which appear to be weapons, but in fact are look-alike weapons. The policy describes look-alike weapons as objects which appear to be dangerous weapons. Students in possession of look-alike weapons and in violation of this policy could be suspended or recommended for expulsion according to Education Code Section 48900(k), if it is determined that possession is disrupting the educational process or creates an unsafe condition.

Violent Act Notification

Senate Bill 142 was approved by the governor on October 1, 1989. This bill added Section 49079 to the Education Code and requires that a school district shall inform the teacher of every student who has caused, or who has attempted to cause, serious bodily injury or injury to another person. Serious bodily injury is defined in the Penal Code as: "a serious impairment of physical condition, including but not limited to, the following: loss of consciousness; bone fracture; protracted loss or impairment of function of any bodily member or organ; a wound requiring extensive suturing; and serious disfigurement." The Penal Code also defines injury as any physical injury which requires professional medical treatment.

Alternatives to Gangs and Drugs Task Force

Hardy L. Brown, Board of Education member, is the founder of the Alternatives to Gangs and Drugs Task Force. This task force is a group of concerned citizens which includes representation from city government, the schools, the police department, the business community, parents, former gang members, and all ethnic groups within the city who meet to share concerns and develop strategies to attack the scourge of gangs, drugs, and violence which threatens schools and neighborhoods.

A goal of the group is to provide a forum where people from different ethnic and economic groups can exchange ideas and engage in open dialogue as they explore ways to confront the growing threat of gang and drug activity in neighborhoods and around schools.

City government officials, school personnel, and police leaders are interested in hearing from parents, students, business leaders, former gang members, and others as they work together to stem the tide of violence in San Bernardino.

Expelled Pupil Transfer to Another District

The San Bernardino City Unified School District worked with Assemblyman Jerry Eaves in support of AB3794. This bill was signed into law during the summer of 1990. The bill was added to Education Code Section 48915, Subsection 48915.2, which requires school districts to advise parents, guardians, or pupils of their obligation to inform any new district in which the pupil enrolls that the pupil has been expelled for any of four serious offenses identified in Education Code Section 48915. The code also requires the district who expelled the student to send a copy of its reason for expulsion with the records upon request from the new district. The four serious offenses are:

1. Causing serious physical injury to another person, except in self-defense.
2. Possession of any firearm, knife, explosive, or other dangerous object of no reasonable use to the pupil at school or at a school activity off school grounds.
3. Unlawful sale of any controlled substance (drugs).
4. Robbery or extortion.

Student Dress Code

On October 4, 1988, the Board of Education adopted a dress code policy for the students of San Bernardino City Unified School District.

A student may not remain at school dressed in a manner in which his or her clothing or lack of clothing (1) creates a safety hazard of said student or for other students at school and/or (2) when the dress constitutes a serious and unnecessary distraction to the learning process or tends to disrupt campus order.

When a student's dress is found to be in violation of the policy, that student may be required to modify his or her apparel so that it no longer violates the policy or the student may be taken or sent home to change unacceptable dress.

The wearing of gang signs, insignia, and distinctive modes of dress is a violation of the policy on improper dress for students. Gang identification is prohibited on any and all campuses of the district.

On January 9, 1990, the Board of Education approved an addition to the dress code policy which was effective February 6, 1990. This addition states that students will not be allowed to wear hats, including but not limited to, sport caps, on the middle and high school campuses unless those hats are authorized by the school administration and contain only the school logo and/or identification.

For further information, please contact your local school or the Special Services Office at 381-1261.

Graffiti Education

Graffiti is often used as a "gang newspaper" marking territories and announcing names of gang members. Parents, community members, and school personnel must join forces with local law enforcement to stop this vandalism. Gangs must not be allowed to use our properties. The San Bernardino City Unified School District removes any graffiti immediately after it is found on district property and is working with police, sheriffs, and the city to eliminate graffiti.

This type of vandalism is against the law (Penal Code 594). It is also against the law for persons under age 18 to possess a can of spray paint larger than six ounces for the purpose of defacing private or public property.

There are about 150–175 incidents of graffiti per month being removed by the City of San Bernardino, Public Services Department, Street Division. Please report any graffiti that you see throughout your community by calling 284-5045.

Dropout Prevention

All San Bernardino City Unified School District secondary schools have on-site programs to assist students in danger of dropping out.

Middle School Programs

Each middle school provides an alternative studies class for students with severe attendance problems and an opportunity class for students who may be experiencing behavior problems which endanger their academic progress. The 601 Family Crisis Intervention Program, housed at Del Vallejo Middle School, serves students from across the district.

High School Programs

Each comprehensive high school program includes a specific class to meet the needs of students experiencing problems in school. Contact the principal at your school for information.

Sierra High School serves continuation students who may be referred on a voluntary or involuntary basis from their comprehensive high school.

San Andreas High School is a voluntary alternative program involving a work/study program primarily for juniors and seniors.

For further information, call the Alternative Programs Office at 381-1265 to request the Safety Net booklet which gives a more complete report on the Dropout Prevention Programs offered by San Bernardino City Unified School District.

Student Assistance Programs

DARE Program (Drug Abuse Resistance Education) — A cooperative effort between the San Bernardino City Police Department and San Bernardino City Unified School District, the DARE program targets 5th- and 6th-grade students to prevent drug abuse in children.

Here's Looking at You 2000 — This drug prevention education curriculum is in place in grades K-12. It addresses one of the critical health issues of the century, addiction, and focuses on the gateway drugs: tobacco, alcohol, and marijuana. Life skills are emphasized.

Insight Program — Insight is a comprehensive, concentrated program designed to intervene with students dealing with drugs, gangs, and other major issues which interrupt education and success in life.

Natural Helpers Program — The Natural Helpers Program assists friends in helping friends and is based on the premise that students with problems naturally seek out peers whom they trust. Middle school students learn skills to help others more effectively.

Peer Leadership — High school peer leaders trained in communication skills can provide a safe, understanding relationship in which students can share personal situations as well as gain awareness of resources that can provide assistance.

Safe School Programs — Target schools receiving state and district grant funding develop individual school site programs to create a positive school climate and enforce consistent discipline systems to ensure a safe and secure place in which to learn and work.

Alternatives to Gang Membership (The Paramount Program) — The Paramount Anti-Gang Program provides 5th and 6th graders with an understanding of the negative consequences of gang involvement in addition to alternatives to gang membership.

For further information regarding these programs, call the Substance Abuse Office at 381-1268.

Anti-Gang Philosophy — Statements/Activities

Statements

"I believe that street gangs, if unchecked, are a threat to the students in our school system. Judging from news reports from Los Angeles, these gangs threaten the safety, not only of other gang members, but of everyone within the area gangs seek to control. Gangs are also a threat because they facilitate the use of drugs and because they lure young people into their illegal and antisocial behavior.

"Our plans include expanding our knowledge of gangs, their activities, their tactics, and their membership. Our school records will not brand students [as] gang members, but our school police will exchange such information with other law enforcement agencies. Without this step, there would be no way to monitor gang activities. Remember, this will not be "school information" that will remain in a student's permanent file. It will be police information which will remain in the files of the school police for the purpose of monitoring gang activities and to deter the products of gang activities —violence, drug abuse, and disorder. If keeping tabs on gang members or potential gang members now will help a youth from acquiring a permanent criminal record, then I think our gang member identification is, indeed, worthwhile."

> — *Hardy L. Brown, President, Board of Education,*
> *San Bernardino City Unified School District*
> *1987-1989*

"Students cannot learn and teachers cannot teach when they live in fear of physical violence."

> — *Nathan Shapell, Chairman of California's Little*
> *Hoover Commission*

"Children will dress the way we allow them to dress. They will speak the way we allow them to speak. Schools should be institutions that form values, not conform to the attitudes of school children. Schools must be responsible and must accept the responsibility. If we don't, no one else will."

> — *George McKenna, Superintendent of the Inglewood*
> *Unified School District*

Anti-Gang Activities

- San Bernardino City Schools has an ongoing program to discourage students from gang involvement and to assist students who have problems in the use and abuse of drugs and alcohol.

- San Bernardino City Schools has an ongoing policy of cooperating with law enforcement agencies that operate within school district boundaries. This cooperation includes allowing police undercover activities on school campuses designed to identify and arrest people selling drugs on campus or making contact with students for sales off campus.

Dress Code
Las Virgenes Unified School District
Calabasas, California

Dress Code: The general atmosphere of a school must be conducive to learning. If a student's general attire or appearance represents a danger to his or her health or welfare, or attracts undue attention to the extent that it becomes a disruptive factor in the school, the principal or his or her designee will ask the student to make the necessary changes. In the event the change does not take place in the time allowed, the principal or his or her designee will prescribe the necessary action to be taken by the school under the rules and regulations prescribed by the state education code and school board policies. In the interest of health, safety, cleanliness, decency, and decorum among students, the following regulations have been adopted by the Board of Education:

- In general, wearing apparel will be determined at the discretion of the parent. However, at any time when there is evidence that the choice of clothing or a student's appearance endangers the student's health or safety, or otherwise interferes with the educational process and mission of the school, the school will exercise its rights and responsibilities to intervene and take corrective action.

- Students are expected to follow all school rules governing safety in specialized programs that may require the wearing of protective clothing, safety glasses, proper foot protection, or other similar requirements.

- In all matters relating to individual dress and grooming, students are required to exercise good judgment, exhibit responsible behavior, and endeavor to reflect respect for themselves, their school, and their community.

- The wearing of clothing, insignia, symbols, or adornments worn or carried on or about a student which may promote the use of any controlled substance, including but not limited to drugs, alcohol, or tobacco, is unacceptable.

- The wearing of clothing which features offensive and/or vulgar words, pictures, or drawings, or, for the sake of humor, includes phrases of a sexual nature or phrases that have derogatory language regarding a person's ethnic background, national origin, religious belief, sexual orientation, or disability is unacceptable.

- The wearing of clothing which represents any group, gang, organization, or philosophy which advocates violence or disruption, or has any history of violence or disruption of the objectives of the school's instructional programs is unacceptable.

- The wearing of clothing which is unduly revealing or attire which detracts in any way from the educational mission of the school is unacceptable.

The district shall review this policy and any additions or amendments annually with faculty, staff, student government, and school site council. This notification shall be timely, preferably at the beginning of the school year.

Legal reference: 5 CAC 300; 5 CAC 302; 5 CAC 5530
EC: 44806-7; 48900; 48907   Approved: 9/12/91

Acknowledgments

Written, compiled, and edited by Ronald D. Stephens.

Selected components of *Safe Schools: A Handbook for Violence Prevention* were adapted from National School Safety Center publications, including:

School Discipline Notebook

School Safety Checkbook

School Safety newsjournal articles:

- "School safety: Who you gonna call?" Peter Blauvelt. Fall 1990.
- "Designing safer schools." Timothy D. Crowe, Fall 1990.
- "Broadening the scope of school safety." Furlong, Morrison and Clontz. Spring 1991.
- "The drugs stop here." Southwest Regional Center for Drug-Free Schools and Communities. Winter 1993.
- "Gazing into a crystal ball." Mary Tobias Weaver. Winter 1994.

Special thanks to June Lane Arnette who assisted in organizing and editing this handbook.

DID YOU KNOW THAT WE NOW PROVIDE STAFF DEVELOPMENT OPPORTUNITIES?

The National Educational Service has a strong commitment to enhancing the lives of youth by producing top-quality, timely materials for the professionals who work with them. Our resource materials include books, videos, and professional development workshops in the following areas:

Discipline with Dignity

Reclaiming Youth at Risk

Violence Prevention and Intervention

Dealing with Diverse Youth

Catching Kids on the Edge

Conflict to Collaboration

Parents on Your Side

Our current mission focuses on celebrating diversity in the classroom and managing change in education.

NEED MORE COPIES OR ADDITIONAL RESOURCES ON THIS TOPIC?

Need more copies of this book? Want your own copy? Need additional resources on this topic? If so, you can order additional materials by using this form or by calling us at (800) 733-6786 or (812) 336-7700. Or you can order by FAX at (812) 336-7790.

We guarantee complete satisfaction with all of our materials. If you are not completely satisfied with any NES resource, just call us within 30 days and *we* will have UPS pick it up at no cost to you.

	Price	Quantity	Total Price
Safe Schools: A Handbook for Violence Prevention	$25.00		
Anger Management for Youth: Stemming Aggression and Violence	$18.95		
Dealing with Youth Violence: What Schools and Communities Need to Know	$15.95		
Containing Crisis: A Guide for Managing School Emergencies	$19.95		
Breaking the Cycle of Violence (two-video set and Leader's Guide	$325.00		
Breaking the Cycle of Violence Transcripts	$20.00		
What Do I Do When...? How to Achieve Discipline with Dignity in the Classroom	$18.95		
Discipline with Dignity (three-video set)	$385.00		
From Rage to Hope: Strategies for Reclaiming Black and Hispanic Students	$19.95		
Shipping: Add $2.00 per copy (There is no charge when you *include* payment with your order.)			
Indiana residents add 5% sales tax			

TOTAL _____

❏ Check enclosed with order   ❏ Please bill me (P.O. #_____)
❏ VISA or MasterCard   ❏ Money Order

Account No._____ Exp. Date _____
Cardholder_____

SHIP TO:
Name_____ Title_____
Organization _____
Address_____
City_____ State_____ ZIP _____
Phone_____ FAX _____

MAIL TO:
National Educational Service
1610 West Third Street
P.O. Box 8
Bloomington, IN 47402